WHAT IS ECONOMICS?

What is Economics?

John E. Maher

Senior Economist
Joint Council on Economic Education
New York, New York

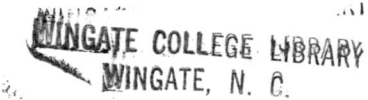

JOHN WILEY & SONS, INC.
NEW YORK · LONDON · SYDNEY · TORONTO

Copyright © 1969 by John Wiley & Sons, Inc.

All rights reserved. No part of this book may be reproduced by any means, nor transmitted, nor translated into a machine language without the written permission of the publisher.

Library of Congress Catalog Card Number: 68-54911
Cloth: SBN 471 56350 I   Paper: SBN 471 56351 X
Printed in the United States of America

Preface

SCORES of people in dozens of school systems throughout the United States and at the cooperating colleges and universities associated with the Developmental Economic Education Program (DEEP) of the Joint Council have contributed to this writing. A detailed list of the Coordinators of economic education and the consulting economists appears in Appendix A. Here I can specifically acknowledge only a few of the people who have helped me in ways too numerous to detail.

Hulda Grobman of New York University read the manuscript, criticized it, and thereby sharpened the focus as only an expert in education could have done. Timely discussions with Suzanne Wiggins of San Jose State College were also helpful.

There is a problem of adequately admitting a vast debt to John D. Lawrence, formerly Director of Curriculum for the Joint Council. It must suffice to say that his knowledge of both education and economics has served both me and the Joint Council long and well and, equally important, his humane, philosophical predisposition has made a delight of my learning about the process of education.

S. Stowell Symmes, present Director of Curriculum, brought his expertise to bear upon the manuscript and thereby rendered great aid. His charm and logic are remarkable.

The President of the Joint Council, M. L. Frankel, provided the aegis of concern and enthusiasm essential to the whole undertaking.

The many economists who replied to the off-beat questions contained in this book were of great assistance to me.

Despite these good people, I may have made mistakes. But the mistakes, if any, are all mine.

JOHN E. MAHER

Contents

Chapter	Page
1. EVER SINCE EVE: AN OVERVIEW OF ECONOMICS	1
2. COPING WITH THIS BOOK	8
3. SOME ACHIEVEMENTS OF MODERN ECONOMICS	16
4. WHAT ECONOMICS IS	22
Five Categories for Economic Activity	22
Relationships	30
The "Optimal" Solution	39
Implications for Teaching and Learning	47
Strengths and Limitations of the Fivefold Division	54
5. WHAT ECONOMICS IS NOT	58
A Matter of Opinion	58
The Topics Dealt With in Textbooks	64
Applied Mathematics	65
Objectives Served by an Economic System	66
General Problem Solving	68
Other Misconceptions	70
6. FREE LIGHT BULBS?	76
Light Bulbs	79
Summary on Light Bulb Policy	93
Note	95

Chapter   *Page*

7. THE ECONOMIC SYSTEM AS A WHOLE   98

    The "Linear" Flow of Income versus the Circular Flow   101
    A National Income Model   105
    What? How? For Whom?   110

8. ORGANIZATION OF ECONOMIC KNOWLEDGE   114

    Mathematical, Classical, and Institutional Schools   115
    Economic Accounting   119
    Conclusion   127

9. THE AIMS OF ECONOMICS   133

    Utility, Pleasure, and Emancipation   134
    The Aims of Economics   137

Appendix

    A   DEEP   149
    B   ECONOMIC KNOWLEDGE (TAXONOMIC)   153
    C   ECONOMIC SKILLS (TAXONOMIC)   160
    ANNOTATED BIBLIOGRAPHY   166
    INDEX   171

WHAT IS ECONOMICS?

CHAPTER

1

Ever Since Eve: An Overview of Economics

EVER since the spell of abundance was broken in the Garden of Eden, individuals and nations alike have confronted the fact of scarcity. It is for this reason that there are economic problems and an economic science. Scarcity means that there are not enough of the goods and services around to satisfy human wants. These goods and services are scarce because the materials from which they are made are insufficient. Thus, there is scarcity of both the resources used in production—land, machinery, equipment, and labor—and the final products into which these resources are transformed. Because of scarcity, there is a need to use to best advantage both the resources and the things produced —to economize. Economics is the science of economizing.

To economize is to choose rationally among the uses to which resources may be put. For the business firms of an economy, the problem of choosing means, in part, decisions about which goods and services to produce—automobiles, refrigerators, miniskirts, hula hoops, appendectomies. It also means choices from among the combinations of resources that will most efficiently produce the goods and services. Whether and how much to use of unskilled labor, automated equipment, acres of land, and other such resources are prime questions. *What* to produce and *how* to produce it are two matters solved by every economic activity.

An economy consists of its business firms and its households. Each household must make decisions as to what it will buy—how it will choose among the goods and services it may purchase. Will it choose coffee or tea? Oleomargarine or butter? A vacation trip or a pine-paneled playroom? How should its consumption expenditures be allocated?

Households and individuals have another set of decisions to make. How will they participate in the productive process? Where will they offer the labor and other resources they command? Because income goes largely to those whose resources are employed, the question, to whom will income be distributed, is answered in relation to the employment of resources.

The power of economic analysis to sort out the interrelationships between production and consumption depends upon viewing human behavior systematically from the viewpoint of scarcity. Whether we talk about a whole economy, a family, or an individual, economic problems generally reveal the five features of economic activity. *Resources* for the whole economy are labor, land, and capital equipment. These are transformed in a process we call *production* into *outputs* of goods and services—haircuts, automobiles, TV sets, transportation. These goods and services are, in turn, transformed through the *consumption* process into things that fulfill human *objectives* by satisfying human wants.

In more familiar terms, we may speak of the making of valentines in the following fashion: construction paper, scissors, paste, the time of school children, and the supervisory talent of the teacher—these are *resources* for making the *output*, valentines. The actual making of them is a process of *production*. In turn, the enjoyment of these, which is *consumption*, yields to happy parents the *objective* of satisfying their parental pride and, to the children, the pleasure of giving.

When we refer to the economy as a whole, we sort out its major functions into a set of questions. What shall be produced? How shall it be produced? (By "how," we mean what resources combined in what ways will be used to produce output?) For whom will production take place? Whose wants will be satisfied? (Here we must note that not only do individuals express their wishes for the goods and services of an economy through their purchases, but government, too, acting on behalf of its people, directs production through its expenditures and in other ways.)

Economics is concerned with the satisfaction of wants in efficient fashion. But what, we may ask, is an efficient way of producing something? In fact, there is no answer to this question simply because we have to know the cost of attaining an objective before we can judge whether it is worth our effort and, if it is, how we may best achieve it.

The matter of cost brings us to another of the key ideas in economics, namely *price*. Goods and services can be compared because they have at least one common denominator crucial to economics: the denominator of price. For example, a haircut that costs $2 is the equivalent of the cost of six quarts of milk, a half-hour's labor from a carpenter, and eight pounds of manganese. We should never be able to make comparisons among such diverse things were it not for the fact that they all carry price tags enabling us to choose among them.

A second set of relationships, which helps to answer questions of how things can be produced efficiently, is the *production relationships*. We can acquire the excavation for a house, for example, by two hours' work from a bulldozer or a hundred hours of pick and shovel labor, or one second from five hundred pounds of TNT.

A third set of relationships appears in consumption. We might receive equivalent satisfaction from wearing a turtleneck shirt or a knitted sweater. These three relationships (price, production, and consumption) unite the five features of economic activity.

The world of economic analysis is usually broken into two parts called *microeconomics* and *macroeconomics*. The former, microeconomics, deals with relatively small units of the economy and the economic problems associated with them: problems of the individual, the family, the business, or a part of the business. By contrast, macroeconomics deals with the problems of the economic system as a whole. In the latter category are such questions as:

4 WHAT IS ECONOMICS?

What determines the level of national income? What influences the level of employment? Why do we have inflation? Why is there unemployment? What can be done about a deficit in the U.S. balance of payments?

The distinction between micro- and macroeconomics is largely one of viewpoint. But it is an important distinction because analysis may yield different results when applied to small sections of the economy than when applied to the economy as a whole. Some of the differences between micro- and macroeconomic analysis can be illustrated with respect to savings.

If an individual is saving his money in order to retire at a later date or to provide for his children's education, we could predict with confidence that sometime in the future he will have accumulated some funds. If, however, we tried to predict the consequences of widespread saving on the economy as a whole, we would discover that it is *spending*, not saving, that turns the wheels of industry. Widespread saving is likely to produce far different results than does saving by an individual. If, instead of buying merchandise off the shelves of retail stores, consumers put increasingly large sums aside for the future, what will keep the retailer at work? What will keep the factories humming to produce merchandise? In other words, if saving for a whole economy exceeds certain levels, it may cause a decline in economic activity and even lead to depression rather than to an improved future. Indeed, what succeeds as individual behavior may or may not work as well for the economy as a whole.

One way in which an analysis of the economy can be portrayed is to imagine the economic system as a giant vending machine that most people serve in two capacities. On the one hand, they are producers of goods and services and, on the other hand, they are buyers and consumers of these same goods and services. To carry this analogy a little further, we may imagine the following physical activity. As workers, managers, and owners, the producers enter the back of the vending machine for productive labor during the daytime. When the day is over, they receive their pay or profits, go home, take a shower, and walk around to the front of the vending machine as consumers. Putting their money into the front of the vending machine, they receive in return the goods and services they have created during the day.

Now, when the people arrive the next morning as workers in the vending machine, what do they find in the till box? They find the money they have spent earlier as consumers. But suppose they failed, as consumers, to spend a good part of the money they were paid in wages and profits. Would there be less money for subsequent payments to them? There would indeed.

This notion of activity leads to the economist's representation of the circular flow of income. Somewhat arbitrarily, we say that productive activity takes place in businesses (neglecting government for the moment) and that households supply resources to business. We then see a flow of services of labor, capital, and land entering business, and an opposite flow of money payments or income going from business to households. In the other loop of the circular flow we see the goods and services that households buy going from businesses to households, and a counterflow of money expenditure going from households to businesses.

The magnitude of these flows is the national income. Speaking somewhat more strictly, it is the gross national product of an economy. Gross national product, or GNP, is defined as the market value of all the goods and services produced in an economy over a period of time, usually one year. In the United States in 1967, the gross national product was about 800 billion dollars.

Through the idea of circular flow, we can see how an economy attains efficient allocation of its resources. Producers' efforts are directed to those lines of economic activity that consumer spending has made profitable. It is the profit motive in a market economy that leads producers to seek to satisfy consumer wants. Industries in which consumer demand is growing will enjoy rising profits and from their revenues will be able to hire additional land, labor, and capital—resources—to be employed in producing the things that consumers want. Industries in which consumer expenditures are declining will suffer declining profits or losses and will have smaller revenues with which to hire resources. This is the meaning of consumer sovereignty in an economy where consumer expenditures largely determine the composition of production.

Of course, not all resources are directed exclusively in response to consumer expenditures. Government plays an important role, and so do such other organizations as trade unions and business associations. It is easy to see some of the reasons government becomes involved in economic activity. An economic system consisting wholly of free, competitive markets would not provide everyone with the opportunity for a minimum education. Therefore, the government, through the expenditure of revenues from taxation or borrowing, finances public education. National defense, social security, interstate commerce, and poverty programs show other instances where the dictates of the market are not freely accepted and government plays a major role.

Most interesting to the student of macroeconomics is the influence of government—largely the federal government—in attempting to promote economic growth and stability through fiscal and monetary policy. By fiscal policy is meant the regulation of government receipts and expenditures to compensate for variations in private spending so that a more even flow of total spending occurs. With stability and growth in total spending (GNP), stability and growth in overall economic activity may be achieved.

Monetary policy means the management of the nation's money supply by the Board of Governors of the Federal Reserve System. Through variations in the cost (interest rate) and availability of credit, the Board seeks to serve the same objectives of national policy as are served by fiscal policy, namely, stability and growth.

The following are a few of the leading economic ideas.

The fact of scarcity pervades almost all of human behavior: there simply are not enough things to go around to satisfy all our wants. As a result, there is a need to economize in the use of our resources and to choose wisely among the uses to which resources may be put.

Choosing wisely means choosing efficiently. Efficiency here means getting as much satisfaction as our employed resources will permit—and, of course, keeping our resources employed.

Economics views in systematic fashion the attainment of want fulfillment through five stages. First, the employment of the *resources* of land, labor, and capital; their transformation in a process we call *production* into goods and services or *outputs;* and finally, through a process called *consumption*, the transformation of goods and services into *want satisfaction*.

An individual economic activity may be viewed in this way

and through the idea of circular flow the activity of the whole economy may also be summarized. The money value of this flow during a period of time, a year, for example, is the gross national product, one of the key indicators of economic performance.

One of the major roles of government—state, local, and federal—is to modify the operation of markets. Of particular interest to economists studying macroeconomics are the instruments of fiscal and monetary policy. Fiscal policy is largely directed to varying federal taxing and spending to compensate for variations in private spending; monetary policy, to influencing business and consumer spending through changes in the cost and availability of credit—that is, the borrowing of money.

Economic analysis is a powerful discipline enabling the student to recognize an economic problem when he sees one, and to map out more efficiently alternative solutions to it. The ability of individuals to solve their own immediate problems is served by this analysis. So is the ability of a nation to meet issues of national policy. Too many times we have seen societies attempt to impose military solutions on what are essentially economic problems; too often we have seen attempts by societies to impose political solutions upon problems that are essentially economic.

An informed citizenry should be able to make the kinds of distinctions that help to avoid such error. We cannot go back to the Garden of Eden. The fact of scarcity will always be with us. We can, however, live better lives if we can cope with this inescapable fact of life.

CHAPTER

2

Coping with This Book

IN recent years there has been an upsurge of interest in the study and teaching of economics. Following renewed concern on the part of the American Economic Association, the teaching of economics in the colleges and universities of this country has been receiving increasing attention. Professors of economics have begun to show a lively interest in the public schools. Evaluation of high school texts in economics and in other social studies has proceeded apace. Moreover, programs have been launched introducing economic concepts into primary and secondary school curricula, from kindergarten through high school. In many major school systems throughout the nation, economists are working closely with curriculum specialists to enhance economic understanding at all grade levels. Teachers are studying economics prior to beginning their careers, and many who missed this opportunity are now returning to the classroom for instruction. All of this is part of a reawakening to the value of enriching the teaching of social studies through the inclusion of economic analysis.

It is only natural to expect that in such a ground swell of teaching and learning and in the wake of the publication of so much new material on economics there should arise concern about the nature of the economics that is to be conveyed. This concern is nothing new to economists but appears now in a new guise. When the college professor is asked what concepts and what tools of analysis he thinks are most appropriate for teaching in the schools and in public forums, he is at first taken aback by the vigor with which the question is pressed and by the new voices in his audience. He is then forced to rethink his understanding of the structure of his dicipline.

Now, when such rethinking by economists is imperative, distracting pressures towards the pursuit of other objectives are greatest. The demand for the services of economists is high and, considering the sterility that attends most discussions of methodology, the temptation has been to duck the issue of defining the discipline in terms appropriate to a large audience including the schools.

There are additional reasons for the chariness with which most economists approach this task. In the first place, the discipline itself is undergoing rapid change, not so much in its basic structure as in the nature of the applications of analysis to specific problems. Economists who are scrambling to learn the latest twist in mathematics—or at the extreme, to learn how to write programs for an electronic computer—are in no mood to to give their attention to the cries for explicit definition of their science and, if one is to be candid, they are becoming increasingly confused by the task of definition.

On one side, a few economists appear to have been seduced into believing that if economics has not been gobbled up by the mathematics of operations research, it has at least been seriously mauled. Others, impressed by the inability of the discipline to pronounce definitively on specific issues, seem unable to defend themselves against the old saw that economics is a matter of opinion. In a most obnoxious yet amusing saying, we have been told: "If you laid all the economists in the world end to end they would still not reach a conclusion."

Finally, the growth in the size and weight of modern textbooks in economics has increased the likelihood that a clear definition

10 WHAT IS ECONOMICS?

of the discipline will seem well nigh impossible. Included within the covers of the typical text are so many subjects, so many perspectives, and so many different kinds of problems that it is small wonder no one wants to attempt a cohesive framework in which to lodge them all comfortably. /

For all of these reasons, it seems timely to try to set down what economics is and what it is not and some of the relationships it bears to other disciplines. In doing this we should also notice some of the sources of confusion among those who wish to understand the nature of the subject.

The dozen years I have spent teaching economics at several colleges and universities do not qualify me to pronounce authoritatively upon what economics is about. But my recent work has at least exposed me to a whole new range of inquiry. In early 1964 I joined the staff of the Joint Council on Economic Education to direct a five-year, nationwide effort to enrich the curricula of major school systems. In this work I have had the rare opportunity of exploring the meaning of economics with primary school children, high school students, teachers, education specialists, professors of economics, and the public at large.

Many of the difficulties I had anticipated in working with school systems have failed to materialize. First graders *can* learn the idea of the circular flow of income, and they usually have fun doing it, and the teachers enjoy teaching it. I had expected that in some cities the parents would impute political inspiration to the Joint Council's program of economic education. Happily, this expectation was also unfulfilled. The nonpartisan nature of the Council largely explains this.

Only one major and persistent difficulty cropped up again and again with almost all of those engaged in the program. This is the meaning of economics and how that meaning can be conveyed to those who are not professional economists. This little book is my response to the persistent difficulty of saying plainly what economics is and what it is not.

The plan of presentation here is to look very briefly in Chapter 3 at some of the achievements of economics. In a way, these achievements are part of a rationale for the importance of the subject. The test of economic accomplishment is not, however, the contribution of the science to the world of ideas, as significant as such a test might be. Nor is it directly the vital place of economic learning in the education of the citizen of a democracy. The case for economic literacy has already been so expertly stated by others that it needs no reiteration here.* Rather, our notice of achievement has the purpose of showing how our lives are shaped by the economic analysis that shapes social policy. If it is important to know something about a force that influences our destiny, a force over which we can exert some control, then it is important to know something about economics.

Chapter 4 is a statement of what I think economics is. It differs in several ways from statements with which I am familiar. It is general in nature and therefore, I hope, generally useful. The reader will find no special discussion of money, international trade, or any of the areas in which economic analysis is applied. I am not writing a textbook and am not especially concerned with applications. Illustrations of general points, yes; orthodox application, no.

I hope, too, that the treatment of economics adequately reflects my rewarding encounters with educators throughout the country. In reflecting such meetings, the writing also differs from the usual statements addressed only to economists by economists.

Following hard upon what economics is, comes Chapter 5, "What Economics Is Not." It is by outlining some of the more influential misconceptions about the science that we can better appreciate its meaning and worth. Some of the misconceptions will strike the reader as curious and, indeed, so little familiar to his daily life that he wonders why they are even mentioned. I can only urge from my observations that these misconceptions are, hither and yon, damaging the teaching and learning of the subject.

All the pages of this book deal with what economics is, not just the second chapter that bears that title. So in Chapter 6, "Free Light Bulbs?", we try to explain by doing. This chapter brings economic analysis to bear upon the question: Who pays for the light bulbs that a major electric utility exchanges for the burnt-out bulbs its customers bring to its offices? I found this

---

* See, for example, *Economic Education in the Schools*, Report of the National Task Force on Economic Education (New York: Committee for Economic Development, September 1961).

an intriguing question whose analysis conveys substantial economic insight. I hope the reader agrees.

The next Chapter, 7, contains a few remarks about the economic system as a whole, the domain of macroeconomics. The contrast between the kind of analysis appropriate to the whole economy and that appropriate to a part will, I feel, fully justify the commentary on macroeconomics.

Chapter 8, "Organization of Economic Knowledge," sets forth a few alternative ways in which economics has been organized for systematic study. Everything that has gone before has assumed the suitability of the framework set forth in the fourth chapter. Yet there are other ways of understanding the science, and these deserve attention. For some purposes and for some people, the alternatives may be superior to the perspective adopted here.

In the last chapter, entitled "The Aims of Economics," I have attempted to say something about the peculiar virtues of economic study. Difficult as the matter is, it seemed to me worthwhile to try to find out what it is that distinguishes economics from other social sciences. There is no attempt to establish a foolish preeminence for economics but only an effort to find out what relationship this science has to a few other modes of inquiry and in what special ways it may contribute to learning. Much of this writing is tentative and may provoke vigorous dissent. The dissent is to be welcomed since it may help us all to arrive at some reasonable estimate of where economics stands.

At various strategic places in this book, I have placed off-beat questions to stimulate your economic thoughts. Since there are no "right" or "wrong" answers to most of the questions, I hope they prove more challenging than the usual kind. Moreover, the idea of the questions is merely to see whether you are thinking as an economist would think. (To check on the validity of my hunch that economists would answer the questions in special ways, I posed them to a number of professionals. The pattern of their responses is given immediately after each question.) The beauty of this way of asking questions is that it doesn't much matter whether you have ever studied the subject; you are able to see at once if "economic thinking" comes readily. If you have any comments on the questions, I hope you will send them to me.

The interspersed questions are one of several ways in which I have tried to emphasize systematic analysis in these pages. For if there is one trouble common to all the social sciences it is their quality of appearing misty, elusive, unsystematic. Trying to hold them is like seizing Jello.

The authors cited at various points give clear indication of the source of many of the ideas presented in this book. Yet explicit, summary recognition must be given the works of Lionel Robbins, Paul Samuelson, and Joseph Schumpeter. A contemporary economist would have to have been educated in strange isolation to have escaped their influence.

Some of what I have written may answer questions by teachers but will be a source of puzzlement to economists. Other things will ring a bell with economists but will leave unmitigated silence for others. This is not surprising and, I trust, simply means that economists should meet with educators to discover what the difficulties are in teaching and learning this subject.

At a few places in the present writing I have borrowed some lines from my contribution to an earlier piece on economics.*

QUESTIONS

STEGOSAURUS (THE ARMOUR-PLATED DINOSAUR)

In an editorial entitled, "New Attitudes on Auto Safety," the *New York Times* (May 1, 1966) commented on the need for federal legislation to require manufacturers to observe safety standards in making automobiles. The need was underscored by "the slaughter of 50,000 people a year on the highways."

Criticizing the industry's argument that costs must be considered in achieving safety, the *Times* said:

. . . projects such as a crashproof car are desirable. As for the concept of balancing cost versus benefits, as suggested by the industry, this seems a fallacious approach. How arrive at a true balance when human lives are at issue?

---

* *Developmental Economic Education Program*, Part Two, "Suggestions for Grade Placement and Development of Economic Ideas and Concepts" (New York: Joint Council on Economic Education, 1964).

14 WHAT IS ECONOMICS?

In a sentence or two, try each of the following questions. (There is overlapping among them.)

1. What do you think economic analysis would add to the quotation from the *Times*?
2. Is a balancing of cost against benefits "fallacious" as the editorial states?
3. Does the fact that "human lives are at issue" prevent society from reaching a balance?
4. Might it be a good idea to build crashproof cars, like Sherman tanks, so that drivers were nearly immune to injury? (What would be some of the consequences of this policy?)
5. Can you think of other instances where human lives are apparently balanced against costs?

ANSWERS

STEGOSAURUS (THE ARMOUR-PLATED DINOSAUR)

1. Economic analysis would certainly add the idea that the *cost* must be reckoned with in the attainment of highway safety. The *benefit* of saving lives cannot be considered in isolation.
2. As the preceding answer suggests, it is the *N. Y. Times* editorial that is fallacious and not the economist's balancing of costs against benefits.
3. The fact that human lives are at issue would seem in no way to preclude the necessary balancing.
4. If automobiles were built like Sherman tanks, one can be rather certain that the public could not afford to ride around in automobiles. This would not only be a rather monumental inconvenience but it would in the first instance, leave several million people without jobs in the automobile industry, the oil industry, the gas station industry, the rubber tire industry, and a host of other industries. These things are not to be taken lightly no matter how strongly one feels about highway safety. Moreover, one might dread to think how the pedestrian would fare when one of these crashproof cars crashed into him.
5. As all of the preceding comments imply, human lives are balanced in many ways and in many instances. The purchase of an insurance

policy puts some kind of financial value upon loss of life, however inadequate the value may be. Every day, judges and juries in courtrooms throughout the country are awarding verdicts in cases of wrongful death. In these cases, where economists often testify as expert witnesses, the economic value of a man's earning capacity is estimated. Moreover, a municipality that decides that it isn't worthwhile to build an underpass at a railroad crossing is making the decision, consciously or not, that the loss of a life every three years or so is not too high a price to pay for avoiding an expenditure of a million dollars on highway reconstruction. None of this is meant to say that it is a fair, accurate, and finely balanced equation that persons arrive at when they put a price tag on human life. Instead, it is only to admit that most of us are, in one way or another, inevitably engaged in this balancing all the time.

Economists responding to these questions generally touched on the points made above. In addition, some noted the loss of income resulting from the deaths of income earners.

CHAPTER

3

Some Achievements of
Modern Economics

An economy is a wondrous transformer beside which the alchemist's magic is nothing. An economy can transmute automobiles into guns, farmers and craftsmen into soldiers, leisure into work, and a long day's waiting into an evening at the theater. With seeming malevolence it can turn Goldsmith's fair Auburn into a deserted village, forests into stumps, and the rebirth of the countryside into a silent spring.

To create representations of a thing as vast and complex as an economic system is an intellectual accomplishment of the first order. Yet economists, largely in the last few decades, have created such representations. Economists can now draw on their models of the economy to predict and explain how the spending by 80 million workers and several million business firms will be affected if they receive a cut in their income taxes. The economic consequences of a curtailment of business spending on investment can now be foretold with a fair degree of accuracy. And this newfound power of economic science has tremendous implications for our lives. Although we may not be aware of it,

SOME ACHIEVEMENTS OF MODERN ECONOMICS 17

our hopes and fears are significantly shaped by policies pursued under the direction of economic analysis. Businesses, governments, and a host of other organizations decide much of their activity on the basis of this analysis.

It is profoundly possible to discuss the achievements of modern economics in terms of intellectual accomplishments. This exercise in the history of ideas might be attempted without special concern for their policy implications. After all, the idea of a circle would be a first-rate one even if the wheel had never been invented. However, we shall not undertake the formidable task of discussing economics in terms of its historical place in human understanding, but rather, by narrowing the range of inquiry, consider chiefly the effects of economic analysis upon social policy. While reflections on the import of economics to policy involves judgments, it is safe to say that people both within and without the profession are compelled by the evidence to agree that the substantial advances in the service rendered by economics to public policy show deep insight into the nature of this most complex of systems: the economy.

One of the most striking accomplishments has been in understanding the modern banking system (although it is true that some marked improvements in banking policy anticipated the theory that later provided their rationale). In the first three years of the Great Depression, which began in 1929, there was a total of 9000 bank failures. At that time there was disagreement among economists as to the causes and consequences of so many failures and confusion over what could be done to end them. The public's savings were largely wiped out and their confidence in the economic order severely shaken. In large part this failure showed that banking was not widely understood and that public policy was not soundly conceived. The Board of Governors of the Federal Reserve System, the managers of our money matters, was relatively impotent; and thousands of banks, faced with tremendous withdrawals, had no alternative but insolvency and failure.

Since the 1930's there have been so few bank failures among members of the Federal Reserve System that you can count them on your fingers. The Federal Reserve is now able to provide the cash needed by banks to satisfy public demand. The satisfaction of this demand is accomplished in seemingly simple fashion: banks can now borrow cash from the Federal Reserve or they can sell bonds to them in exchange for cash. While the mechanics of this operation appear to depict a rather simple institutional change, it is only possible because of a greater understanding of the complex role of monetary policy in the economy and an understanding of the consequences of changes in the supply of money. The Federal Reserve now manages our money supply, its expansion and contraction, in such a way as to make major contributions to economic stability. The public, whose faith in banking has been largely restored, would feel even more secure if it better understood the operation of a modern banking system.

Greater strides than those in money matters have been taken in fiscal policy—the management of federal taxing and spending—as a direct result of the analysis and measurement of national income. It is difficult today to appreciate the gap in economic knowledge that existed just a few decades ago. In the nineteen-twenties there was no working *definition* of national income. There could, therefore, be no *measurement* of it; and there could be no operational theory, no *explanation* of why income went up and down. In this plight, sound economic policy to attain high levels of national income and employment was, to say the least, difficult to devise.

Recent years have been marked by a generally satisfactory set of answers to these questions of definition, measurement, and theory. Indeed, the government's fiscal policy is largely built upon this triad. Whether it is tax cuts, budget deficits, or the balance of payments, economic policy is solidly based upon an analysis of effects on the nation's income. Economic growth and much of our competitive coexistence with the Soviet Union are understood principally in terms of income analysis.

Most recently and so less securely entrenched in economic science are the wage-price guideposts suggested by the President's Council of Economic Advisers during the Kennedy administration. Seeking to foster price stability, the Council urged that wage increases be kept approximately within the bounds set by productivity increases for the economy as a whole. Most simply stated, if workers have generally produced about three percent

SOME ACHIEVEMENTS OF MODERN ECONOMICS 19

more this year than last year, then an increase in wages of about three percent will not raise costs per unit of output. Hence, since costs will not rise, prices need not rise. Guideposts for price changes have been developed in roughly similar fashion.

Now, while a particular figure like three percent may be hard to defend, this guidepost was based on an analysis of the operation of the economy and the historical trends of wages, prices, employment, and income. And, until 1967, the government's unprecedented policy showed signs of influencing major collective bargaining negotiations throughout the country. Although the guideposts have now been largely abandoned, they nevertheless revealed an important use of analysis in the formation of policy.

The contribution of economics to national security has been remarkable. From among the many illustrations in this field, we may here notice the use of the so-called "input-output" analysis developed by Wassily Leontief.

Suppose the United States government wishes an answer to the question: What is the most sensitive place in the economy of a potential enemy? The purpose of getting an answer may be the preparation of plans for bombing or missile attacks in the event of war. The reciprocal question for the defense of our own industries is equally interesting: What is the most sensitive place in the American economy? What economic activities should be most heavily defended?

For any economy, this question raises innumerable possibilities. Are oil wells the most sensitive area? Steel mills? Munitions factories? Railroad yards? Which of these, if crippled, would most impair the operation of the economy, particularly its war-making potential?

The input-output analysis referred to above provides answers to these questions. It shows each industry's economic connections with other industries, thereby putting into relief the interdependence of all economic sectors. It shows to what extent production in other industries will be affected by impairment of production in a particular industry; it reveals, as well, the total effect upon the economy.

The military application touched on is only one use of the concepts of input-output; military procurement is another. And peaceful uses are equally significant. Yet the one illustration given above suffices to show another value of economic science for public policy.

There are other important applications of new economic findings to questions of public policy. These include foreign trade, economic growth and development, and the importance of government regulation on the economy.

In concluding this brief treatment of a few areas in which economics has shown substantial progress, we shall mention some applications to problems of business.

Certain kinds of business problems had for years resisted any solution but the time-consuming and costly method of trial and error. Trials were numerous and errors were multiple. This was true of the problems of inventory control, traffic regulation, transportation and communication analysis, and a host of others. Since World War II, however, economic analysis—in company with modern mathematics and the high speed computer—has succeeded in devising methods for arriving at good solutions to many of these hitherto intractable problems.

Only a mature discipline could have reached the position occupied by economics in public and private councils. This degree of maturity shows most distinctively in the large consensus represented by modern economics textbooks. There is not one kind of income analysis in one text, another in a second, and so on. Rather, there is substantial agreement among virtually all. The college courses entitled "Principles of Economics" all seek to convey the same body of doctrine, the same principles.

The situation with respect to other social sciences and history is markedly different. There are textbooks, to be sure, but they do not agree in their representations of a common body of thought. And to the extent that they do agree, it is not on fundamental principles but very often only on their discussions of the leading historical figures who contributed to their discipline. Thus, nearly all texts in political science will deal with the writings of Plato, Aristotle, Hobbes, and Machiavelli. But on what common body of principles will they agree? What are the principles of political science? Of sociology? Of history? That there are some generally accepted principles, no one can deny, but that there are enough of them to constitute a body of scientific knowledge is open to doubt.

None of this, of course, detracts from the importance of the other social studies. Indeed, it might well be argued that the lack of an accepted orthodoxy makes their study all the more worthwhile since truth in these areas is a more elusive creature. The only point in contrasting the greater maturity of economics with allied disciplines is to note the particular values attached to an appraisal of it.

Another way of stressing the achievement of economics is to note that, as a *system* of principles, it applies powerfully to the understanding of its "real-world" counterpart, an economic system. Throughout these pages I have tried to bring out this kind of systematic inquiry.

The achievements of modern economics mark the discipline as one of the most advanced of the social sciences, yet it remains a field of study obscured from much of the public. Neither the public nor the public's elected representatives can be fairly expected to support sound economic policies unless the analysis upon which the policies rest is vigorously advanced in the schools and colleges. The following chapters are a contribution to this advancement.

CHAPTER

4

What Economics Is

FIVE CATEGORIES FOR ECONOMIC ACTIVITY

Most people know that economics deals with such items as population, natural resources, incomes, tariffs, money, and prices. Indeed, the list of topics can be greatly extended.

However, it is not *what* economics deals with that makes it a distinctive science. Instead, it is *how it organizes and analyzes* its materials, the perspective from which it views the world, that make it a special field of study.

To show that it is organization and analysis rather than the subject matter itself that set economics apart from other studies, we need only reflect on the fact that sociology is equally concerned with population and natural resources; political science, with incomes and tariffs; history, with money and prices.

Economics is a particular view of reality. From this view, human behavior is seen as activity directed toward the achievement of various objectives through the use of various resources. As tentatively depicted in Figure 4.1, resources (means or instruments of achievement) leads to objectives (aims or ends). The *process* by which resources lead to the fulfillment of objectives is called production.

Economics is a particular angle from which things are viewed. Consider a simple event like the loading of fuel, ammunition, and food aboard a Navy ship. If we imagine all this cargo piled up on a dock, we avoid the complicated problem of selecting cargo and can concentrate on the simpler matter of studying the process of getting the goods on board.

What is it we see when looking at a ship being loaded with stores? Superficially, we see some men leaving the ship, filing along the dock, picking up a variety of things, and carrying them back on board. Other men with pencil and paper appear to check the proceedings. Still others seem to stand idly by. The men who are doing the manual labor are generally a little dirty and more poorly dressed. The ones who do the checking are cleaner but also poorly dressed. The ones who stand around watching are cleaner and well dressed in uniforms that sparkle with golden emblems.

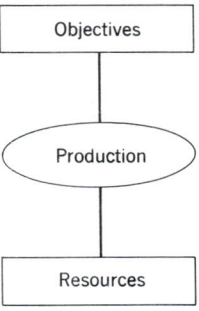

Fig. 4.1 Economic activity (tentative depiction).

This cursory description of the process of ship loading is what is meant by "sheer description." It analyzes nothing, it explains nothing. Like a mirror, it merely reflects what is taking place. And like a mirror it contributes nothing to one's understanding of why things take place. The why of things requires analysis.

The economist might begin his analysis of this event by assuming the *objective* or purpose of the activity to be the loading of the ship within a given period of time using as few of the men (*resources*) as necessary. The process of loading is a process of production. That is, the process aims at producing a ship loaded with stores. In carrying out his analysis, the economist has to be guided by a knowledge of important relationships. For example, a sailor will break his back if he tries to pick up two five-inch projectiles; if a projectile is dropped on its nose, the production process may be brought to a thunderous end; and if first-class petty officers are given the dirtiest jobs of loading, their efficiency will be nil.

Now, this same loading activity may be viewed by a sociologist (or political scientist) from a different standpoint. The focus of sociological analysis might be on identifying the *authority* that governs the crew's behavior. It would be noticed, for example, that men in the Gunnery Department are in charge of stowing the ammunition; those in Engineering are in charge of fuel; those in Supply, in charge of food. Within each department, work is supervised by rank and rate, the officers overseeing the chief petty officers, the chiefs overseeing the rated enlisted men, and so on down the line of command. This is the hierarchy for the execution of orders.

This case in sociology is not so trivial as may at first appear. To the extent that *special knowledge* rather than *rank* is the basis for authority, the flow of orders may even go from a third-class petty officer to a commissioned officer. This will commonly happen when the latter does not know enough about the task to be able to issue appropriate orders. To carry this observation to the apex of authority, it may be pointed out that the captain of a ship is much more in command of communications and gunnery than of engineering, simply because of his knowledge of the first two and his ignorance of the last. If the Chief Engineer tells the Captain it will be six hours before the ship can use its number two generator, the Captain will, however reluctantly, accept the situation. Typically, he knows little or nothing about generators. But if the Gunnery Officer says the ship cannot fire its main battery of guns, there will be a lot of explaining to do, and the Captain will have innumerable suggestions for setting things aright. The Captain knows something about gunnery because such knowledge is traditionally a prerequisite to promotion to command.

A final view of this activity of loading a ship is that of the physicist or engineer. One of the important considerations for an analysis of the physical loading of heavy objects is the effect upon the stability of the ship. If it is to remain upright in the water, the symmetrical placement of stores is essential. If the ship is to be able to weather rough seas, there is a specific limit to the weight it can carry.

The purpose of considering at some length this little Naval exercise is to show a few of the various perspectives from which different organizations may be made of the same basic materials. Of even more importance, however, is the demonstration that, generally speaking, the things we observe in the world are not to be divided into those that are economic, those that are sociological, or political or engineering. Rather, almost all events have an economic aspect, a sociological aspect, as well as many others. Only by recognizing that different disciplines are generally different points of view can we successfully avoid mistaking a *discipline itself* for its *applications*. Only in this way, too, can we appreciate what gives to a problem its economic coloration.

Economists have long recognized that it is not a particular kind of human behavior that is to be called economic in nature. Rather, it is the angle from which any behavior is viewed. As Lionel Robbins observed:

> The conception we have adopted may be described as *analytical*. It does not attempt to pick out certain *kinds* of behavior, but focuses on a particular *aspect* of behavior, the form imposed by the influence of scarcity. It follows from this, therefore, that in so far as it presents this aspect, any kind of human behavior falls within the scope of economic generalizations . . . . There are no limitations on the subject matter of Economic Science save this.*

With this general conception as our starting point, we protect ourselves from the error of thinking that there are major institutions and organizations in society that are economic—business firms and labor unions; others that are political—the Congress and Supreme Court. Instead, we see that there are economic and political aspects to virtually all institutions and organizations.

Another vital point that the quotation from Robbins brings into the discussion is "the influence of scarcity." Economics is the study of that aspect of human behavior shaped by the influence of scarcity. We need to state more exactly what this influence is.

Neither an individual, a family, a business, nor a nation can readily attain all of its objectives. Considered from an economic perspective, the chief reason for this near impossibility of com-

---

* *An Essay on the Nature and Significance of Economic Science* (London: Macmillan & Co., Ltd., 1962), pp. 16-17.

plete attainment is the scarcity of goods and services. Roughly speaking, there are not enough things to go around—not enough food, clothing, shelter, medical services, education, leisure, or other valued items. And there are not enough of these things we call consumers' goods and services because there are not enough resources out of which such goods and services are made—not enough, relative to the wants the resources may fulfill. This relative scarcity of resources is the basic fact that causes human behavior to show an economic aspect. People generally have to behave in a special way; they have to "economize" because of scarcity.

Now, what does it mean to economize? It means, generally, to meet the problem of scarcity by making rational choices among the alternative uses to which we may put our scarce means, our goods, services, and productive resources. We do not have enough of the scarce means so we must choose rationally how we use them. For an individual or family, the choice of putting time, money, and other scarce means into a vacation at the seashore may mean foregoing a new automobile. For a business, the choice of installing new machinery may mean doing without a new home office building. For a nation, the choice of increased armaments may mean giving up a better educational system. For virtually every society and throughout all history, the influence of scarcity has given human behavior a special, economizing aspect.

Economics, then, is that point of view from which human behavior appears as activity directed toward achieving various objectives using various resources. The objectives may be the social goals of national policy like full employment of the labor force; or, in smaller-scale problems, such goals as a new suit of clothing or a pencil sketch of an elephant. Similarly, the resources employed to attain the objectives may be such broad resources of the economy as land, labor, and capital; or, at the individual's level, an hour's exertion, a piece of paper and a pencil. In all cases, scarcity prevails: there are simply not enough resources to satisfy all objectives. From this wide range of objectives and resources, it is clear that economics is concerned with both individual and social problems. Thus, the emphasis upon economics as a social (societal) science should not obscure its usefulness for the study of smaller problems (microeconomic problems) of the individual, the family, or the business firm.

We are now in a position to change our earlier statement and diagram of economic activity to show two additional things. First, what we usually get from a productive process is not the direct achievement of our objectives, but rather various kinds of goods and services. These goods and services that productive activity puts out, we call *outputs*. Second, in most cases it is necessary that the outputs be used in *consumption* before we attain our objectives. Indeed, it is the satisfaction of our wants that is our objective, and consumption is required in order that wants may be satisfied.

Figure 4.2 has been drawn to show these two additions to our earlier formulation of economic activity. Now, in between "Objectives" (or Satisfactions) we place outputs and consumption.

Interpretation of this diagram will clarify its use. Reading from bottom to top, we start with resources: the land in a pea patch together with the farmer's labor, his shovel, his hoe, and some seed are *resources*. (Sunshine and rain are resources too, but the farmer has little control over them nor does he pay to use them.) Next, the *production* process includes plowing, planting, weeding, and harvesting the peas. The *output*, of course, is peas—if everything has gone well. But a bushel of peas is not the end of the whole activity. Rather, the satisfaction of hunger is the objective. For this satisfaction to take place, another process intervenes, namely, the process of *consumption*. When the peas are consumed, the *objective* is satisfied.

There are millions of ways of illustrating the processes of pro-

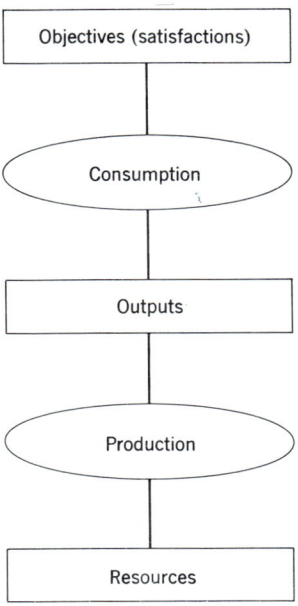

Fig. 4.2 Economic activity in five parts.

duction and consumption. We could have used the steel, glass, labor, and machines that are some of the resources used to produce automobiles. The driving of the automobiles is then the consumption that satisfies the public's objective of locomotion. Perhaps better for showing the generality of this scheme is the following example. Three hours of a student's time, coupled with his knowledge, a paper, and a pencil are resources for producing the output known as a completed examination and a grade on the report card. His and his parents' objective of having him become a well-educated person will (ostensibly) be satisfied through the pleasure of poring over his report card and enjoying his learned company. (We assume the student to have behaved in so efficient a way as to get an impressive grade.)

Selected chiefly for pedagogical convenience, the five parts into which economic activity is divided are resources, production, outputs, consumption, and objectives (satisfactions). As a rough generalization, we may say that resources and outputs are often fairly concrete things (although a surgical operation, for example, is an output that is not material); satisfaction is a psychic phenomenon, difficult to measure; and production and consumption are transformation processes. In the first, production, resources are transformed into outputs; in the second, consumption, outputs are transformed into satisfactions.

QUESTIONS

PROCESSIONAL

1. How would an economist be likely to explain the connections among the following things: Labor, capital, technology, economy, ginger ale, and thirst?

2. Column A repeats the six things mentioned in question 1. If, in answer to question 1, you have these six as part of a single system, try to make a similar system of all the phrases in Column B.

    In the space appearing before each phrase in Column B, write the word from Column A that most nearly corresponds to that phrase.

    You will notice a word left over in Column A. See if you can "invent" a good corresponding word phrase for a match in Column B.

WHAT ECONOMICS IS   29

Column A	Column B
1. Labor	———— Henry Wadsworth Longfellow
2. Capital	———— "The Children's Hour," a poem
3. Technology	———— Poetry
4. Economy	———— Imagery, metaphor
5. Ginger ale	———— Longfellow's knowledge of language
6. Thirst	

ANSWERS

PROCESSIONAL

1. Labor and capital are two resources which may be combined in a production process to yield the output, ginger ale. Technology consists of the ways in which labor and capital may be combined. Economy is the use of efficient means of production. Thirst is the want satisfied through consuming the output, ginger ale.

2. The six items in column B can be arranged in a system closely parallel to that discussed for the items in column A. Longfellow's exercise of poetic skill (labor) combined with his knowledge of language (capital) yield the "The Children's Hour," a poem (an output analogous to ginger ale in column A). The technology or methods by which this is achieved is through the use of imagery and metaphor. The criterion governing the writing is poetry (economy). The want that is satisfied by this output could be, perhaps, one or both of two things: Longfellow's desire for fulfillment and the public's thirst for entertainment.

The following is a list of these six correspondences. The figures before each item show the percentage of economists who agreed with this rank. The only items of moderate disagreement are 4, Economy, and 3, Technology.

90	1. Labor	Henry Wadsworth Longfellow
66	5. Ginger ale	"The Children's Hour," a poem
48	4. Economy	Poetry
63	3. Technology	Imagery, metaphor
70	2. Capital	Longfellow's knowledge of language
70	6. Thirst	*Desire for fulfillment* (by Longfellow) or *Public's thirst for entertainment*

RELATIONSHIPS

What is it that unites the five parts of economic activity? As suggested in the diagrams above and in the accompanying discussion, there are connections among all the parts. These connections are the *relationships* that, when taken together, form a *system* of the whole. What, then, are these relationships?

To identify those that are important in the solution of economic problems, we need to set up a little example slightly more complicated than those heretofore dealt with. Let us assume that we have as an objective the satisfaction of our want to travel by automobile. The output which will satisfy this want is a moving car. The production that will produce this output is a car, burning gasoline as we drive down the road. The resources that we need to achieve this production are gasoline and an automobile (and such other things as license plates and our own ability to drive).

The initial complication that we now set forth is that the resource, gasoline, is divided into one gallon of regular gas and one gallon of premium (higher octane) gas. This difference between two resources suggests one of the most common relationships, namely, that which tells us how much of one resource is the equivalent in production to how much of another. If a gallon of regular gasoline is equal to four-fifths of a gallon of higher octane in moving an automobile, then it is clear that in purely technical terms, the higher octane gasoline yields twenty percent more mileage. Here, then, is a production relationship.

Let us assume with respect to production that it takes one gallon of regular gasoline to move the car twenty miles and only four-fifths of a gallon of a higher octane. In Figure 4.3 we see the relationship between the consumption of a gallon of regular gasoline and the output of locomotion represented by the label on the arrow at the left as one gallon yielding twenty miles. The relationship between higher octane gasoline and locomotion is shown by the arrow on the right and the label, one gallon yielding twenty-five miles.

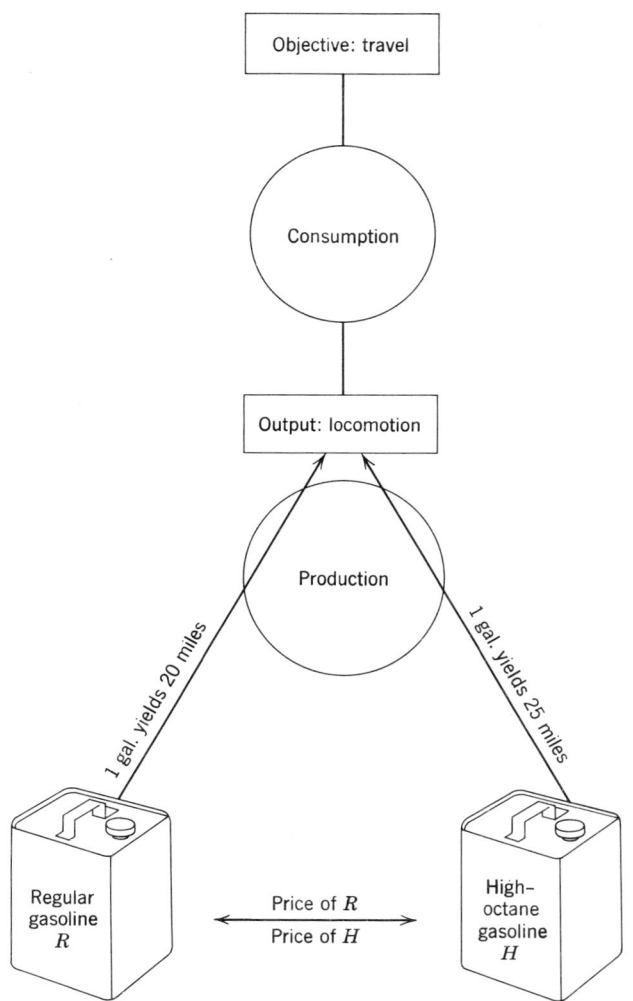

Fig. 4.3 Economic activity involving a choice between two resources.

We see immediately that there is no basis for deciding which kind of gasoline we will use. If they cost the same amount per gallon we should obviously prefer the higher octane that carried us farther. But if the higher octane is much more expensive than the regular, we should prefer the regular. Therefore, a second kind of relationship is required for the solution of this problem, namely, the price of each. Price is a market relationship, in contrast to the production relationship cited earlier. Once we have the price of each gasoline, we will know which one to prefer. In this example, we find that if the higher octane gasoline costs up to twenty-five percent more than the regular gasoline, it will be more economical to use the higher octane. Otherwise, the regular is to be preferred.

At this point, it should be emphasized that beside the five parts of economic activity that we have identified and the relationships that bind the parts together, it is necessary to have a guiding *principle* in order to govern the entire *system*. It will be noticed that the principle of "least cost" was the guiding consideration in our solution of the problem of choosing between two gasolines. Thus, for example, given all the facts just mentioned, we would not be able to say that the higher octane gasoline would be preferred if it cost less than twenty-five percent more than the regular if we were told, in addition, that we must not use high octane gasoline because it is too inflammable. So we need a determining principle for rational decision making. We need a guiding criterion for *optimizing*. The most common expression by economists is, indeed, optimizing, which means finding the "best" solution to a given problem subject to the conditions under which the economic activity proceeds. We shall later wish to examine more closely this highly restricted definition of the word "best," since great care must be exercised in the use of so superlative a word.

In order to display other relationships that are usually intrinsic to the solution of any economic problem, we must consider the case in which there is more than one objective to be served. Thus, imagine that this time we have two objectives that we may achieve through the use of gasoline, a single resource. First is the enjoyment of a mowed lawn (provided we own a gasoline driven power lawnmover) and second, a trip in our automobile. For the satisfaction of each of these objectives there is an associated output. The first output is a mowed lawn; the second output is locomotion. Figure 4.4 depicts this situation of one resource which may be used to serve two objectives.

Now if we *already have* the gasoline on hand (so we may ignore the cost of its acquisition), we may decide that we want a little of both objectives, depending upon the *amount of satisfaction* that will be yielded by the achievement of some of each of them. But if we think that a mowed lawn is much more important to us (yields more satisfaction) than does a trip, we may decide to put all of the gasoline into the operation of the power lawn mower.

We see from the line connecting the two objectives that each of them yields satisfaction and so each is, to some extent, a substitute for the other. If we know the consumption relationship between the satisfaction of the two objectives, we can decide how much of the resource to devote to the attainment of each.

Another way of answering on slightly different grounds the question of which objective to satisfy is to assume that the gasoline carries a price tag of, say, 35¢ a gallon and that we have not yet acquired it. Now, if it takes a gallon of gasoline to mow the lawn and also to make the trip, we may have a way of measuring directly the relative advantage of using the gasoline for one purpose or the other. Thus, if one of our children will mow the lawn with a manual mower for less than 35¢ and there are no other costs involved, it would be foolish for us to use the power mower and, therefore, purpose one is ruled out as uneconomical. Similarly, it might be stated that if we could make the trip on a bus for less than 35¢, we would not acquire gasoline for this purpose. If both these conditions hold, then we don't buy the gallon of gasoline. Of course, these kinds of "solutions" assume that we do not care about the difference in the appearance of the grass when it is mowed by one machine or the other and that we consider a ride on the bus as convenient as a ride in a car. Only the different money costs associated with these outputs are explicitly taken into account here.

Two relationships, then, may unite the component parts of this economic activity into a single system: (1) the amount of

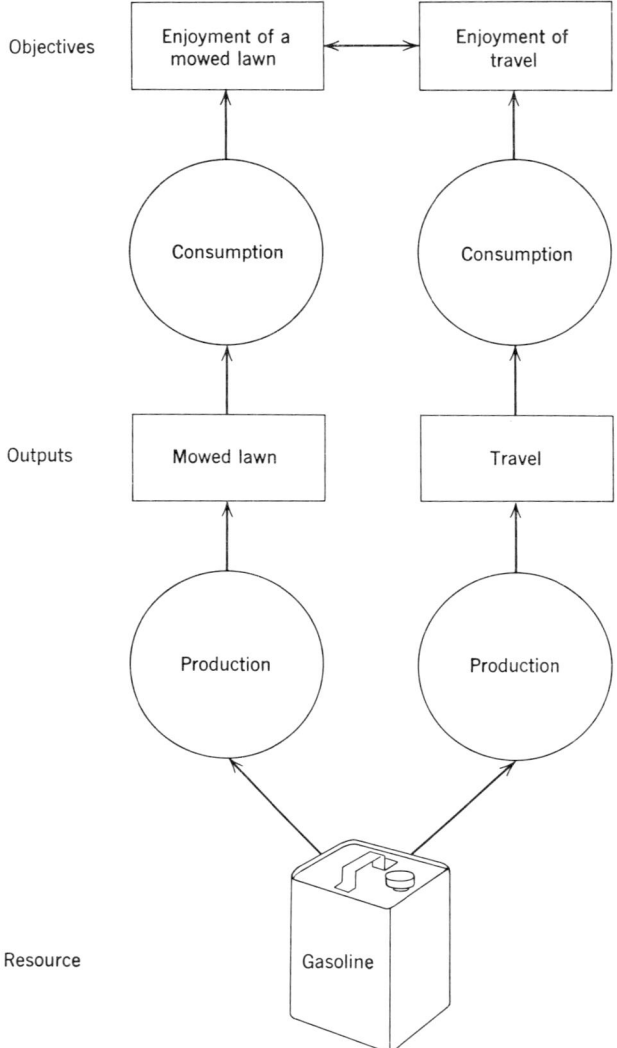

Fig. 4.4 Economic activity involving one resource and a choice between two objectives.

satisfaction that will be yielded by the devotion of a resource to the satisfaction of the objectives and (2) the price tag we attach to the outputs that are possible from the uses of the resource.

The name "opportunity cost" is given by economists to the satisfaction foregone by the employment or use of a resource in a given endeavor. Thus, the *real* cost to an individual of using gasoline to ride around in his car may be the lost opportunity to enjoy a nicely mowed lawn. Now, it might be thought that, generally, a person can have both. But, on the contrary, even though he may satisfy several of his wants, it generally remains true that his resource could always have been employed to satisfy a different want. Therefore, there is (almost) always an opportunity cost to the use of a resource. We cannot have our cake and eat it too: what we choose to do now precludes our doing something else.

An individual who spends his vacation in Bermuda cannot also spend it in the Rockies; a family that uses its savings to educate the children cannot also use the same savings to buy a new house; a nation that puts most of its national budget into national defense cannot also put most of its budget into education. Choices must be made. And the real cost or sacrifice made in choosing one option is the satisfaction that could have been derived from choosing the next preferred alternative.

QUESTIONS

CONSUMPTION

A person must choose for his dinner either Menu A or Menu B, as shown below. He does not have to pay for his meal and he may eat as much as he wants from the menu he selects.

Which menu will he choose and why?

Menu A	Menu B
Mixed Fruit	Strawberries
Soups du Jour	Chicken Rice Soup
Seafood Platter	Lobster Newburg
Homemade Pies	Pecan Pie
Coffee, Tea, or Milk	Coffee

ANSWERS

CONSUMPTION

At the outset we may assume we are dealing with the "average" or "typical" person, a highly elusive creature found mostly in advertising studies. Of course, I have no more idea than the reader whether such a person will prefer Menu A to Menu B. Someone might say it depends on which main course is to be preferred and, therefore, you cannot answer the question until you know whether the average person prefers a mixed platter of seafood (Menu A) to lobster newberg (Menu B).

Because the answer to the question cannot be made to hinge on the unknown preferences of the public, the thing to do is to look for differences between the two menus. Their striking similarities are obviously not going to provide any basis for distinguishing them. The only characteristic I see in which they differ is that Menu B in every case gives *no choice* while Menu A in every case gives a choice; therefore, assuming people like to choose among several things, the preference is for Menu A.

There is another, more important, reason for urging the preference for Menu A, and that is the fact that in all instances Menu A may include what Menu B has on it. Thus, the mixed fruit may contain strawberries, so that you get in the appetizer from Menu A what you get from Menu B, and you get *more besides*. Similarly, the seafood platter may contain lobster newburg so that Menu A is better in that it includes what is on Menu B for entree and *more besides*. Finally, the desert, beverage, and soup on Menu A may well include what is on Menu B.

Now, if you agree that Menu A may well have on it everything appearing on Menu B and, in addition, other good things, then Menu A is to be preferred.

While a few economists wrote that the question could not be answered, most of them made a choice. Of those who chose, 79 percent picked Menu A.

We may now summarize what we have said about the identification of relationships that bind the parts of economic activity together into a cohesive whole. In summarizing, we shall introduce more than the few relationships dealt with in the preceding illustration and in this way achieve a greater degree of generality.

Price relationships: Resources (inputs) on the one hand, and goods and services (outputs), on the other, are related to each other by three *price* relationships. (1) The prices of resources tell us how much we must sacrifice of one resource in order to obtain quantities of another. (2) The prices of outputs tell us which output will more economically satisfy our objectives. (3) The prices of resources (inputs) compared with products (outputs) tell us whether or not it is worthwhile devoting a resource to a particular line of production.

Production relationships: There are also three sets of what we may call *substitution* relationships. First of all, in the productive process, one resource may be better at yielding output than another, and the relationship of the production to be had from one resource as contrasted with another tells us which is the more technically efficient.

Technical efficiency must not be confused with economic efficiency. The former term refers to the physical relationships among resources and outputs. Consider the manufacture of fountain pens from two metals, gold or steel. We might be able to get just as many pens (output) from a pound of either of the two metals (resources). So the *technical* efficiency, the relationship between the number of pens produced and the physical quantity of metal used, might be the same whether gold or steel were used. But in economic terms, the efficiency is different: the cost of steel is so much less than the cost of gold that steel is the more *economically* efficient metal. When economists talk about the substitution of one factor of production for another, they generally have in mind only those factors that are economically feasible.

Closely related to the substitution of factors of production is the celebrated law of diminishing returns. This law states that if larger and larger quantities of one resource are combined with a fixed amount of another resource, a point will be reached where output will increase by smaller and smaller amounts. The law assumes that technology, the techniques of production, is unaltered.

A rough illustration of this law may be drawn from the coal

mining industry. Imagine that an employer is increasing the number of workers (the labor resource) employed in the mine (land resource). The coal mine is the resource held constant in amount; labor is the resource whose employment is increasing. Technology, the method of digging coal, is unchanged. Initially, as more workers are sent down into the mine, more tons of coal are dug. At first, a doubling of the number of miners may double the output of coal. But a point will be reached when an increase in the number of miners will lead to a less than proportionate increase in the number of tons of coal mined. Then we say that diminishing returns has begun to take effect. Eventually, of course, the number of miners may become so large and conditions in the mine so crowded that any increase in employment would lead to a decline in the output of coal.

The law of diminishing returns has been tested empirically for a few productive processes, notably in agriculture. But its validity rests largely on the following kind of abstract consideration: if production from a fixed resource could be increased endlessly by increased employment of a variable factor, then it should be possible to grow the world's food supply in a flower pot! It would simply be necessary to add fertilizer (or labor or some other resource) in extremely large quantities.

In this brief discussion of the substitution relationships among factors of production, special attention has been paid to the law of diminishing returns. This is because the law is believed applicable to virtually all productive processes. Moreover, it serves as a good explanatory theory of why production is carried only to certain levels in various industries and firms. The student who pursues the study of economics very far soon learns that the assumption of diminishing returns underlies an important part of the explanation of competitive business.

Consumption relationships: Other substitution relationships are the substitutions of outputs in consumption. We may use butter instead of oleomargarine. We may watch television instead of going to the movies. Here, the satisfaction we derive from goods that are substitutes for one another may vary as we go about the process of consumption.

There are other relationships that emerge as we go more deeply into the analysis of economic activity, particularly as we develop more complex systems. It is sufficient at this point to have shown some of the interconnecting relationships among the five components categorized earlier.

For a particular problem, the five categories already enumerated together with the relationships that bind them may be called a *system*. It is clear that a system may be a very small thing, as in our earlier illustrations of the use of gasoline to achieve locomotion; or a system may be a very large thing as illustrated by the whole economic system which is the sum of all the resources, all the productive activities, all the outputs, and all the relationships of the total economy.

THE "OPTIMAL" SOLUTION

The "rational" operation of any system requires a guiding criterion, and we call adherence to this guiding criterion, efficiency. We may define efficiency as the allocation of our resources in that fashion which permits the greatest achievement of our objective. When we have achieved our objective most efficiently, the system is said to be optimized.

The idea of the efficient allocation of resources is enormously important. And one of the most useful forms of this idea is expressed by economists as "equilibrium at the margin." We need to explore this matter briefly.

Suppose there is a student who wishes to get as good an *average* grade as he can in the study of two subjects, mathematics and literature, for example. He has at his disposal a certain number of hours each week in which to study the two subjects. He believes that if one hour of study is taken from mathematics, his semester's grade will fall by one percent; if that hour is devoted to the study of literature, his semester's grade in that subject will rise by two percent. Clearly, he should shift the hour's study from mathematics to literature and thereby raise his net overall grade average by one percent.

Again, the reallocation of another hour taken from mathematics may drop his grade in that subject by one-half percent; applied to literature, the grade there may rise by three-quarters

40 WHAT IS ECONOMICS?

percent. So this further reallocation is "profitable," yielding a net gain in the average for the two subjects of one-quarter percent.

Now, how far should this process of reallocation continue? How many hours should be allocated to literature rather than to mathematics? The answer obviously is: hours should be reallocated to literature until the loss in grade average in mathematics is equal to the gain in grade average in literature. Then there will be no further advantage in taking more time from mathematics.*

Stated differently, an "equilibrium" in maximizing the average of the two subjects is reached when the loss at the margin is equal to the gain; that is, when the last (marginal) hour devoted to the study of each subject yields the same increment to the grade. Of course, this principle can be generalized to apply to any number of subjects.

While I should dislike making fine calculators out of students or their teachers, the matter of equilibrium at the margin is of such wide application that it is worth a graphic treatment. Figure 4.5 shows the change in grade in each of the two subjects associated with an hour's study of that subject. We assume there are ten hours to be allocated during a week. As an illustration of the reading of the graph, we look at the column where 4 hours are devoted to literature and 6 hours to mathematics. We read directly above these two figures that the change in the grade in

---

*What does the economic advice mean when we say the student "should shift an hour's study from mathematics to literature?" Does it mean that economists favor literature over mathematics? No, indeed! Anyone who has read the writing of economists knows that their bias is in quite the opposite direction. Rather, the advice simply means that if we accept as fixed the student's objective of raising his grade average by allocating a certain number of hours of study, then it follows that he "should" shift an hour from one subject to another, since his gain in grade will exceed his loss. Thus, it is the *student's assumed value system* to which we are adhering. We have assumed that he wants to raise his grade average.

The role of values is obviously of great importance to the attainment of the good life. So, too, is the role of economizing. But values may exist largely independently of the economizing process. The economist, therefore, is in no special advantageous position to declare what values a person or society ought to pursue. With respect to the illustration above, most educators would agree that students' pursuit of high grades is a major stumbling block in the whole process of education.

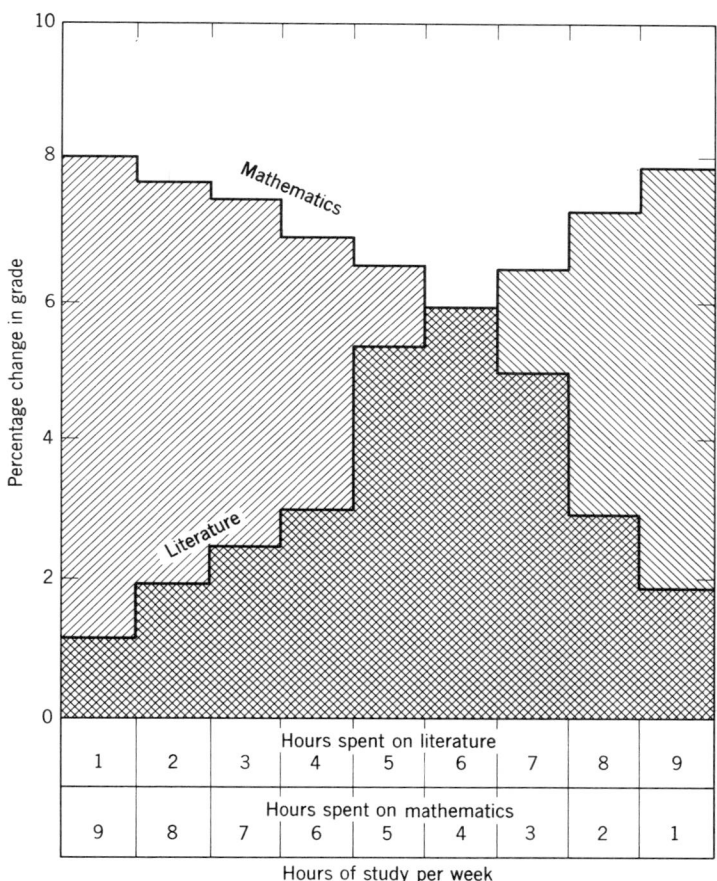

Fig. 4.5 Allocating ten hours' study to maximize the average grade in two subjects.

literature is 3 percent, the change in math, 7 percent. This is a total change of grade of 10 percent. Now, considered by itself, this position does not tell us much. But if we compare this with the one labeled "optimal allocation," we can see that improvement is possible. At this second position, with 6 hours on literature and 4 on math, the respective changes are both 6 percent for a total of 12. By adding two more hours to literature we have gained 3 percent (from 3 to 6) while the loss to math is only 1 percent (from 7 to 6).

Hence, again, we see an illustration of opportunity cost. The cost (sacrifice) of a better grade in literature is a poorer grade in mathematics—and vice versa. And if someone said, "Why not put more time into the study of both subjects?" we should point out that something else would have to have less time devoted to its pursuit. More hours of study might mean less sleep, fewer social engagements, a loss of time before the television set. Just what would be given up, we do not know. But some opportunity would be foregone. This is the meaning of the inescapable and pervasive opportunity cost.

This same procedure of weighing alternative uses of resources pervades economic analysis. Whether it is assigning workers to this task or that, substituting machinery for labor, producing one product or another, selling in one market or another—in all of these cases, marginal analysis is essential. Moreover, as the preceding detailed example is meant to suggest, the usefulness of this approach extends far beyond what we typically think of as economics. In principle we can and do weigh other kinds of alternatives in similar fashion: in love, life, and labor, such balancing is often appropriate. Finally, of course, we note once more that marginal analysis can include scores of alternative uses of resources; it is rarely restricted to just two.

There is need for particular attention to the word "rational" in the definition given earlier to the effect that the rational operation of a system requires adherence to a criterion of efficiency. All solutions of economic problems are subject to conditions of various kinds. Now, the conditions themselves may or may not strike our fancy as being particularly rational. In India, for example, where the standard of living in many areas is low, we might consider the religious belief that prevents people from consuming cattle as an "irrational" condition under which production and consumption take place. People of Eastern cultures might similarly contend that the Western world's working only an eight-hour day and not generally working at all on the Sabbath is also an "irrational" limitation upon production and consumption. The use of the word rational here, however, refers to the achievement of a "best" solution, accepting as given the limitations or conditions that are posed as part of the problem. It is not the conditions to which the word rational applies; it is, instead, the logical observance of the conditions. This is the sense in which the word "best" is used in economics. It is always a limited or constrained best solution that economists put forward, for economics is the science of the conditional and the contingent. It does not deal in superlatives; it has no truck with idealistic utopias. It is a distinguishing mark of the science that it has accepted expulsion from the Garden of Eden and knows full well that man must earn his living by the sweat of his brow or, at the very least, under natural and social conditions that are not easily altered.

We may contrast this realistic acceptance of the conditions of life by showing a noneconomic approach to a question that, properly construed, can certainly be made to yield to economic analysis. Suppose someone says he wants the "best possible education" and then asks, "How can I get it?" A flippant answer dealing in superlatives, might be this advice: study for ten years each at Harvard, M.I.T., Michigan, Berkeley, Oxford, and Cambridge; then study for twenty years at the Institute for Advanced Study, five years at the Center for the Study of the Behavioral Sciences, and eight years at the Congressional Library. This adds up to ninety-three years of study.

What is wrong with this answer? Nothing. It is the question that is at fault, for no one expects the best possible anything. Humanity is constrained to live within various limitations. Our appetites are limited; we cannot study endlessly; we do not live forever. We must eat, sleep, and play. We cannot afford, for these and other reasons, to devote all our resources to the attainment of any single objective. As a consequence, the question, "How may I obtain the best possible education?" needs severe qualification. While we cannot attempt it here, an answer can be devised to such a question as this: given my interests, aptitudes, intelligence, age, income, and family responsibilities, how may I obtain the education most satisfactory to me?

While we should never stifle the superlatives of poetic license, it is probably better to control their flights in analytical discussions. Otherwise, analysis becomes ambiguous parable. By way of illustration, the following advice to teachers is cited.

44 WHAT IS ECONOMICS?

If these data are to be useful to teachers in planning learning experiences to meet the individual needs of the students in their classes, they ought to have in their possession *all pertinent information* about the students *they can possibly obtain.** (Emphasis added.)

All pertinent information . . . they can *possibly* obtain? Fingerprints? Blood type? Family tree? Coats of arms? Should those who gather such data also have in their possession the biggest file cabinets they can possibly obtain? And the largest warehouses and the greatest staff of file clerks? But enough! The writers of this exhortation got carried away by their enthusiasm for research. They could never have intended that busy schoolteachers should drop everything else and devote their lives to gathering data about students. In economic terms, the objective of getting data on students can reasonably be reached only by economizing on the resources at one's disposal. Among the resources is the time spent by teachers gathering data. One doesn't want all he *could* acquire, and no one would want to spend all his time in this pursuit.

At a later place we shall return briefly to the theme that economic thinking is usually more efficient if extreme, superlative notions are avoided. There we shall take up a questionable proposition that has pervaded much otherwise sound economic discussion, namely, the proposition that the central economic problem arises because human wants are unlimited. Now we shall take one more look at "superlative" thinking.

This time we choose a formulation of the central political challenge facing Western civilization. Our spokesman for the Western world is Otto Butz, an outstanding political scientist, who, in a series of unconstrained exhortations, poses the dilemma of modern man.**

Butz begins by stating as his purpose the stimulation of the

---

* "Working Paper on Evaluation of Learning," Allen, Dodds, Hanna, and Taba (Washington, D. C.: n.d., mimeographed), Association for Supervision and Curriculum Development, NEA. I realize, of course, that if enough burden is placed upon the word "pertinent' in the quotation, then the interpretation I make in the next paragraph is weakened. How much better (not best) to have urged simply that teachers get that pertinent information to which they may reasonably be expected to have access.

** *Of Man and Politics* (New York: Rinehart & Company, 1960).

reader "to reflect upon those (political) facts in their most meaningful possible philosophical, historical, and analytical contexts" (pp. v-vi). He later represents the inspiration of the Western world view as the "philosophy of maximized secular welfare" and asks how else one can understand man's attempt "to devise the most efficient possible mechanisms of production and distribution in the interest of the greatest achievable common good?" His answer is "the enthronement of the ideal and practice of the greatest possible secular well-being as the highest modern absolute" (p. 16). And then we have "civilization's most fundamental and universal challenge: *how to organize man's greatest possible welfare as a member of society, while leaving him with the greatest possible moral autonomy as an individual human being*" (p. 18).

Now, our purpose in citing at some length the writing of a political scientist is not to take issue with political science. Rather it is to contrast one mode of thinking with another, one example of political theorizing with what we have said is characteristic of economic theorizing. To the economist, the phrase "greatest possible" is almost devoid of meaning because it suggests a violation of the human condition, a devotion of all resources to the achievement of one end; it denies the economic problem of choice and conflict among competing ends. Moreover, to suppose that man can pursue *two* ends to the "greatest possible" extent—be they welfare and moral autonomy or whatever—is, in an economic perspective, self-contradictory. You cannot eat all your cake and retain it too. Eating and retaining are processes leading to opposite results, namely, not having and having.

The point bears reiteration: among all the social sciences, economics is preeminently occupied with solving problems under strictly constrained circumstances. The economic view of reality has much to contribute to other views, chiefly for this reason.

QUESTIONS

OPTIMIZING

In solving problems, economists seek a best or optimal solution. What do they mean by the words "best" and "optimal"? Put a "one" in the

46 WHAT IS ECONOMICS?

space after the phrase you think most nearly conveys what they mean, a "two" after the next most nearly correct choice, and so on until you have ranked all four phrases.

By "best" or "optimal" solution, economists mean:
The very best possible solution obtainable   ———
The solution that yields highest profits   ———
The solution that yields lowest costs   ———
The solution reaching the objective with
  fewest resources   ———

ANSWERS

OPTIMIZING

First choice:
"The solution reaching the objective with fewest resources."
This seems to be the best answer because it is nearly a definition of optimal. If you get one objective with the fewest resources, then you have the most resources left over for the attainment of other objectives. It follows that you can obtain more of your objectives by employing as few resources as necessary in the attachment of each.

Second choice:
"The solution that yields highest profits."
This is the second best answer and applies to many kinds of public and private activity. Business firms are guided by this notion of optimal and so also may be private individuals, households, and even certain government activities whether or not they are classified as profit making. Even in the Soviet Union, where they do not speak about profits as readily as we do, one still finds that a factory manager seeks to have a large "surplus" of revenue left over after meeting the costs of production. This is the second best answer, however, because there are many, many instances where the concept "profit" has little application. A worker who takes one job over another can't very well say that he's trying to get the highest profits because there is no easy way of defining the cost which would be deducted from his receipts in order to arrive at profits. Moreover, there are activities, particularly in the public domain, where the concept is not applicable. The building of highways, the construction of hospitals, and the running of a poverty program do not easily lend themselves to this conceptualization.

Third choice:
"The solution that yields lowest costs."
This would seem to be a third ranking choice for the meaning of "optimal" for several reasons. One is that lowest cost is often reached by not doing anything at all. If you want to cut your cost of travel to zero, you can simply choose not to travel. If a business wants to cut its cost of production to zero, it may be able to do so by producing virtually nothing. If production is the objective, it is therefore not attained at lowest cost. An equally good reason for not ranking this choice very high is the fact that it provides no measure of gain from an economic activity but only the cost of resources employed. This is a grave deficiency. Something that costs very much but yields a high reward is considered a good thing. We can not look at cost alone to determine whether an activity is being run in optimal fashion.

Fourth choice:
"The very best possible solution obtainable."
This notion of optimal or best is really without what scientists call "operational significance." It has little or no useful meaning. As illustrated elsewhere in these pages, to get the "very best possible" anything implies devoting all your energy and resources to its attainment. This might, indeed, yield a result that appears *in itself* very satisfactory, but the costs are enormous. Thus, if I want to become proficient in the Russian language, I may spend all my waking hours studying the reading, writing, and translation of Russian. I may become highly proficient, but I won't be able to do much of anything else. The impairment of my ability to do anything else is too high a cost to make this an optimal solution.

Economists responding to this question gave the same ordering as discussed above. The percentages of responses are as follows:

1. The solution reaching the objective with fewest resources.   60
2. The solution that yields highest profits.   45
3. The solution that yields lowest costs.   35
4. The very best solution possible.   50

IMPLICATIONS FOR TEACHING AND LEARNING

I have made no attempt to spell out in detail, as one would do in a textbook, the depths of analysis and the richness of problems characteristic of economics. Nevertheless, from the preceding discussion of the structure of economics, there should be implications for teaching and learning. If we have succeeded at all in laying bare the structure, there must be implications for how this structure may be interpreted to those who would learn about it.

The five numbered points that follow are not a rigid sequence of steps to be taken in learning and teaching the subject. Rather, they are groupings of instructionally related themes: (1) economics readiness; (2) component categorization—the five-fold scheme adopted here; (3) relationships; (4) the combining of components and relationships into a system; and (5) the economy as a whole (the subject of Chapter 7).

1. As a first observation we might note that since economics is one of the behavioral sciences, the students' readiness for economics (economics readiness) means the same thing as "science readiness"; that is, following current educational thought, the students' readiness for learning science is a readiness for learning economics.[*] Generally speaking, we mean familiarizing the students with: units of measure and their relationships, the indirectness of scientific information, the need for operational definitions of ideas, the confrontation of hypothesis with fact, and the notion of multiple causality among physical and social phenomena.

2. Beyond ascertaining science readiness in conveying the structure of economics, we must categorize in particular ways. By this we mean delineating some arrangement like the five parts of economic activity: the definition of resources, production, outputs, consumption, and objectives (satisfactions). It is possible, of course, further to categorize these five components and, as Table 4.1 shows, there are several bases for categorization.

Most generally, as is shown in columns 2, 3, and 4 of the table, we can note that for these five components there are such mutually exclusive divisions as between public and private; between scarce (costly) and free; and between durable and nondurable. It is perhaps stretching the applicability of some of these dichotomies to apply them to all five categories, and yet we know

---

[*] Jerome L. Bruner, *The Process of Education* (New York: Alfred A. Knopf, Inc., and Random House, 1960).

Table 4.1 Economic Categorization of Activities

Five Parts of Economic Activity 1	Dichotomies 2 3 4			Illustrations 5
Objectives (satisfactions)	Complementary Competitive			(Love and marriage) (War and peace)
Consumption	Individual (appendectomy) Family (house) Community (playground, school) Nation (national defense)			
Outputs	Consumption Investment Government Foreign investment			Goods Services — Industries, e.g.: Automobile industry Coal mining industry Laundry industry Tourism
Production	Agricultural Nonagricultural			Manufacturing Nonmanufacturing — Goods Services
Resources	Owned property Human labor			Land, including mineral resources Labor — Occupations: barber, doctor, carpenter, shoe salesman Male-female White-nonwhite Skilled-unskilled Production-nonproduction (i.e., supervisory) — Capital Enterprise

Column dichotomy headers (rotated): 2 — PUBLIC (COLLECTIVE) VERSUS PRIVATE; 3 — SCARCE (COSTLY) VERSUS FREE; 4 — DURABLE VERSUS NONDURABLE.

Illustrations (Outputs): Goods (and services) may be complementary in consumption: ham and eggs; nuts and bolts. Or they may be competitive: butter and oleomargerine; coffee and tea.

that they fit pretty well. As the large column 5 to the right shows, each of the five categories may be further subdivided in various ways. Some of the most common of these are shown in the table.

We need perhaps only pause here to notice that in the row labeled "outputs" we see, first, a fourfold division. In this case the division is aggregate output for a whole economy: gross national product. Here are listed consumption, investment, government purchases, and net foreign investment. (One of the many uses to which this particular fourfold division may be put is spelled out in Chapter 7.) Here as elsewhere, we may refer to the most succinct discussion of the meaning of these important economic concepts, namely, that by Professor James Calderwood.*

3. Following categorization we have the identification of relationships. These were earlier discussed and consist chiefly of price, technical substitution, and consumption relationships. Table 4.2 sums up and illustrates these major relationships.

4. The fourth step in the process of defining the structure of economics is the combining of categories and relationships into a system. (This was discussed in the immediately preceding section.) Along with the idea of system comes the criterion of economic efficiency in the obtaining of objectives and the optimal nature of solutions to economic problems.

5. Lastly, in the process of getting at the structure of economics is the highest level of aggregation (macroeconomics) in which is studied the operation of the entire economic system—the sum of all the production and consumption activity as registered in such aggregate measures as national income, the general level of prices, the average wage level, and the size and composition of the labor force.**

---

* James D. Calderwood, *Developmental Economic Education Program*, Part One, "Economic Ideas and Concepts" (New York: Joint Council on Economic Education, 1964).

** The study of aggregative relationship is a major branch of economics that has been given little attention so far in these pages. The reason for this slighting includes the need to economize on time and space and the belief that, in principle, the economy as a whole is comprehended from the same perspective already developed here with important modifications. It must be emphasized that the transition to the analysis of the whole system is fraught with difficulty. Therefore, macroeconomics rightfully holds a separate and important place in the study of science and is treated, below, in Chapter 7, "The Economic System as a Whole."

Table 4.2 Economic Categorization of Relationships

Relationships	Illustrative Examples (Hypothetical, Only)
Prices	
Of outputs	An egg sandwich costs half as much as a ham and egg sandwich.
Of resources	A ton of coal costs two-thirds as much as a ton of oil.
Of outputs compared with resources	A barrel of crude oil costs a fifth as much as five gallons of gasoline.
Substitution	
Of outputs	An egg sandwich is only a quarter as satisfying as a ham and egg sandwich.
Of resources	A ton of coal yields four-fifths the heat derived from a ton of oil.
Of resources in supplying outputs	A barrel of crude oil yields twelve gallons of gasoline.
The law of diminishing returns applies to both consumption and production relationships.	After repeated or prolonged viewing, a person may get fed up with watching television.
	With known technologies one cannot grow the world's food in a flower pot or bathtub.

This order of presentation of the structure of economics—categories, relationships, subsystems, and aggregate system—defines the necessary order in which these ideas should be studied and developed in no precise manner. It is true that the easiest thing to teach and learn is probably a simple categorization while, at the other extreme, the most difficult is teaching and learning about the aggregate economic system. But in between these two extremes, there is room for wide variation. Some problems in categorization are very difficult indeed and require the most mature consideration on the part of adult minds. On the other hand, some problems of relationships and of simple systems can easily be grasped and, in fact, are being grasped in the public schools at the level of kindergarten and first grade.

The following list summarizes a way in which economics may be learned and taught. Except for the first point, science readiness, the list is a reiteration of the structure of the discipline.

1. Science readiness
    Example: units of measure, the indirectness of scientific information, operational definition of ideas, testing hypotheses with factual observation, the notion of multiple causality of events.
2. Categorization
    Resources, production, outputs, consumption, and objectives (satisfactions).
3. Identification of relationships
    Price relationships among outputs and resources. Substitution relationships among resources in production and among outputs in consumption.
4. Combining categories and relationships into systems
    Attaining the "optimal" operation of a system requires a guiding criterion of performance.
5. The whole economy as a single system.

QUESTIONS

MEANS AND ENDS

Among the many loose sayings (usually offered as criticism) by which we try to guide our personal conduct and, often, our national conduct, is the adage:

The ends do not justify the means.

Economics is especially concerned with this very relationship of means and ends. Through economics we are *helped* to discover whether or not the ends justify the means.

For each of the following four statements, identify the means (things used and resources employed) and the ends (purposes and objectives) and check the space telling whether *you* think the ends justify the means employed. (In one of the statements, no apparent means are specified.)

	The means are:	The ends are:	Do you think the ends justify the means: yes or no?
1. The problem of alcoholism would be completely eliminated if the death penalty were imposed for all people caught drinking, buying, selling, or possessing alcoholic beverages.	___	___	___
2. People know the causes of air pollution, but little is being done to control it.	___	___	___
3. American automobile manufacturers know how to build crash-proof automobiles, but they are not building them despite 50,000 highway deaths a year.	___	___	___
4. Despite what many think is proof of the deadly effects of smoking cigarettes, million of people continue puffing away.	___	___	___

ANSWERS

MEANS AND ENDS

1. The end or objective in this statement is the solution to the problem of alcoholism. The means employed, as stated, is the imposition of

the death penalty for anyone trafficking in the beverage. I think the ends do not justify the means.

2. The end or objective in this statement is the elimination of air pollution. The means are not specified but could include regulation of automobile driving and of engine construction and prohibition of irresponsible burning of trash as well as control of smoke emissions from manufacturing plants. Here I think the end justifies more means than are currently devoted to it.

3. The objective here is the reduction in the number of highway deaths. The means suggested is the construction of crashproof automobiles. As discussed in these pages, there are reasons for my belief that the ends do not justify the means, as valuable as human life is.

4. This is the most difficult of these four statements because, unlike the first three, this one really seems to be directed toward the satisfaction of the smokers. It is therefore not a highly respected and socially approved objective. Specifically, the end or objective is some kind of satisfaction (narcosis) which people who smoke cigarettes achieve through the means of tobacco. Smokers tend to think the ends justify the means but nonsmokers don't.

Most responding economists gave answers like the ones above. A few were uncertain about several of the statements. The widest variation in reply was whether the reduction of disease or smokers' satisfaction was the objective implied by statement 4.

STRENGTHS AND LIMITATIONS OF THE FIVEFOLD DIVISION

There is, of course, a danger that generalizations about the nature of economics or of any other field of inquiry will be interpreted in exaggerated fashion. Economists are no more nor less prone to push their ideas forward with messianic zeal than are disciples of other persuasions. Karl Marx, of course, comes readily to mind as an economist against whom the charge of intellectual imperialism has been leveled fairly.

The division of economic inquiry earlier set forward is not some magic key to unlock all the riddles of economic behavior but is a help to teaching and learning. To the extent that this paradigm is a key, there are interesting doors whose locks it will not fit. Then, too, there are doors which may be opened only to reveal empty rooms on the other side; that is, there will be instances where a problem can easily be understood within this economic scheme but where, at the same time, the results of understanding turn out to be trivial or vacuous.

We should not, however, underestimate the value of such broad generalizations as the ones with which we have been concerned. Problems of the individual lend themselves to analysis in the terms we have considered. Whether a person has as his objective the building of a birdhouse or the budgeting of his income, for a variety of purposes it will often be found that our scheme may yield significant results. Of course, results will never be more significant than the problem to which the scheme has been applied.

At another level of complexity, the family and its economic behavior will be found amenable to this outline of economic activity. Indeed, we should expect that wherever there is an *economizing problem*, these insights should prove valuable. There is great formal similarity between the problems of the individual and those of the family. Both have objectives; both are consuming units; both require goods and services for consumption; both are generally engaged in production; and both require resources. Here, of course, production includes not only the generation of income through paid employment but also the goods and services resulting directly from family and individual activity.

Most useful is the application of this framework to an exploration of the productive processes of a business or firm or a part thereof. A department or division of a business can readily be brought within the scope of inquiry.

Further levels of aggregation are the industry—a collection of firms engaged in producing the same product; a sector of the economy, for example, the business sector or government or households; a region within the nation like the Pacific Northwest, which may, because of the common resources and markets it touches, be thought of as a single unit; or the whole national economy.

It is also necessary to add that in certain important cases, some of the components of this fivefold division blend smoothly and instantaneously into one another. An opera singer performing before an audience, for example, is producing something of value for the patrons who have paid to hear her sing. She is producing something of value through the rendition of a song. The patrons are consumers of the song at the instant of its production (neglecting the time it takes for sound to travel). And their objective of hearing music is being satisfied at the moment of the production and consumption of this service. Needless to say, there may be lasting values—the memory of an outstanding performance—which will continue to satisfy them and therefore fulfill their objective long after the last high C has been sounded.

Another point to notice is that some outputs from a productive activity are inputs to another productive activity. Thus, for example, we may think of labor and sand and machinery as some of the resources going into the glass producing industry. The output of this industry may be window glass for automobiles. This output, of course, is an input to the automobile industry, and the output of the automobile industry is an input to the industry that consists of car rental agencies; and so it goes. Therefore, no product is necessarily an output (or input) from all points of view. The issue is decided by the perspective we adopt.

Moreover, certain outputs from the entire economy (those called capital goods, in particular) are classified as "final" outputs but, because they last a long time, they render services (inputs) to later productive activity. For example, the diesel locomotive is classified as a final output. Yet, as is true of all capital goods, its function is to render services that will be useful in further production. The diesel locomotive that hauls people and freight over the rails is rendering service to the railroad industry for an indefinitely long period of time.

Another point, like the preceding, arises from the fact that some objectives that are "ultimate" for one person or organization are instruments or means of achievement for other persons or other organizations. Going to church may be a means to salvation for some parishioners while it may be an end in itself for others. Again, the miser who hoards his money may be seen as appreciating money, not for its value in acquiring this world's goods but rather as a nearly "ultimate" objective in itself.

Thoreau, in his classic book, *Walden,* displayed this point quite clearly when he considered that in building a house it may be that *efficiency,* in its ordinary meaning, is not particularly desirable. "It would be worth the while," he wrote, "to build still more deliberately than I did considering, for instance, what foundation a door, a window, a cellar, a garret have in the nature of man, and perchance never raising any superstructure until we found a better reason for it than our temporal necessities even. There is some of the same fitness in a man's building his own house that there is in a bird's building its own nest." Here, among other philosophical implications, Thoreau suggests that the economic advantages to specialization in having carpenters and other craftsmen build one's house may entail wrong values. He implies that, like birds, man by nature may serve himself better by laboring for himself in providing his shelter.

CHAPTER

5

What Economics is Not

THE preceding chapter attempted to formulate a positive statement of what economics is. The present chapter is a cautionary one whose moral is: Beware of the dogma, dressed in economic clothing, that is not economics.

At the outset we deal with five different misconceptions that masquerade as economics. These misconceptions pretend that economics is:

1. A matter of opinion
2. The topics dealt with in textbooks
3. A branch of applied mathematics
4. The objectives served by an economic system
5. General problem solving

We shall look at each of these in turn.

A MATTER OF OPINION

Those who do not know much about economic science are fond of saying that, after all, economics is a matter of opinion. A person who advances this view usually holds strong minority convictions on issues of great economic importance. Since he is profoundly innocent of any knowledge of the subject, his convictions are anchored to the wind. The only way he can get his unsound opinions accepted is to argue that economics is a matter of opinion and his opinion is as good as anyone else's, particularly an economist's.

Legitimate controversy over economic policy is invigorating both to economics and to public policy. Both benefit from the discoveries that such controversy engenders. But the mistaken notion that the science *is* opinion is invariably based upon crass partisan interest. And the motives of those who espouse the notion are like those of a man who argues against the legal sale of alcoholic beverages while he is operating a bootleg distillery.

An illustrative case is the director of a nonprofit "educational" organization in the West whose ostensible purpose is economic education. He holds to the "opinion school" and adds to this opinion the doctrine that government cannot (by definition?) do anything economically productive. The rationalization behind this wrong-headed doctrine is simply that, since whatever government does is financed by taxing or borrowing from "the people," it is "the people" who are always the agents of production, not the government.

Now the same argument can as easily be applied to business. Whatever production a business engages in is financed by money spent by "the people" on purchasing the commodity sold by the business, or it is financed by borrowing from "the people." But this whole question of who finances production is quite beside the point. The real question in the view of an economist is whether or not goods and services get produced because of some agency like government or business. And the answer must be that goods and services are so produced. Production by business is obvious enough. So, too, is the production for which government is responsible: schools, hospitals, roads, research, national defense, and the operation of the legislative, executive, and judicial systems.

No organization is *solely* responsible for the production in which it engages; and no measure of productive value, in dollar terms, accurately reflects all costs and benefits. But the value of the productive contribution of government is recognized, though understated, in all data on national income. No economist denies this fact.

What our opinionated friend is really saying to his audiences is this: Economics is a matter of opinion, and my opinion on the subject is as good as an economist's. One of my most cherished opinions is that government is generally too meddlesome in economic affairs. The businesses who finance my propaganda share my views, and it will make them and me happy if you will believe me when I say that government cannot produce anything. Then you will help me to curb the government.

The opinion school has, unfortunately, received support from the unguarded statements of highly respected businessmen. Thus, Bernard Baruch is quoted as saying, "If they (economists) knew so much, they would have all the money and we would have none."* This view, of course, misconstrues both the purpose and the substance of economic analysis. It is like saying that if doctors knew so much about medicine, they would have all the health and the rest of us would have none. It is perhaps unnecessary to add that the purpose of economics is not to enrich economists any more than the purpose of medicine is to promote the health of doctors; a lack of income is as much a subject for inquiry by economists as the lack of health is for doctors.

The notion that economics is a matter of opinion is sometimes given apparent foundation by disagreement over matters of public policy. Of course, the good society as envisaged by the National Association of Manufacturers differs from that sought after by the AFL-CIO. The utopia of the Republican Party differs from that of the Democrats. It follows that spokesmen for each group, including economists, often have different objectives in mind and therefore often advance different economic policies (as well as different political and social policies). This must be accepted as a matter of different objectives or sometimes as a different understanding of the facts or a different interpretation of their implications. It is rarely, however, that one could, upon close scrutiny, find that the different pronouncements stemmed from a different conception of what the nature of economic

---

* C. Wright Mills, *The Power Elite* (New York, Oxford University Press, 1959), p. 351.

science is. The language of economists is the same in no matter whose employ, and so are the general principles of analysis. Only in certain rather advanced fields of study, like the ultimate factors accounting for the stucture of interest rates over time, are there apt to be professional differences of opinion among economists. And these differences, we may be assured, do not generally influence the course of day-to-day disputations.

There is, of course, a healthy decline apparent in the appeal of this specious view that economics is a matter of opinion. Certainly, all sectors of the economy—business, labor, and government—are anxious to recruit economists from whatever reputable universities and from whatever regions of the country. This means that a professional person is sought for his skill and that this skill can be objectively determined. Moreover, the widespread support for economic education from all sectors of the economy suggests that the supporters do not think that there are different brands of economics and that one should be favored and promoted over others. Equally telling is the great improvement in the literature published by special interest groups. With minor exceptions, the analytical quality of special reports issued by the American Bankers Association, the AFL-CIO, and the U.S. Chamber of Commerce is something to be admired.

We may therefore conclude that economics is not a matter of opinion.

QUESTIONS

TRADE

How do you think an economist would rank the following comments on U.S. trade with Communist Cuba? Put the number one in the space before the choice you think an economist would *like best,* a number 6 before the choice the economist would *dislike most,* and so on with the other numbers, 2, 3, 4, and 5.

U.S. exports to Cuba should be:
_____ stopped except for nonstrategic (nonwar-making) materials.
_____ stopped.
_____ permitted.

_____ stopped except in materials that Cuba can acquire from other nations.
_____ permitted when such exports are part of deals by which we get something we need from Cuba.
_____ governed by military policy, not economic policy.

ANSWERS

TRADE

This question is surely ambiguous and there is no single set of responses that is correct, either from the economist's or from almost any widely held point of view. However, there is a preference for certain rankings of answers over others among the majority of economists.

Before giving a "preferred" set of rankings, it is probably a good idea to consider a few basic ideas about trade. Trade between individuals or between nations is a two-way street. One nation has something that another nation wants and vice versa; therefore, exchange is possible. Now, what would probably trouble someone considering this question of U.S. exports to Cuba is the fact that most Americans don't like the government of Cuba. The American government does not recognize the government of Cuba. The Communist ideology dominant in Cuba is antithetical to the ideology of capitalism dominant in the United States. These facts would color almost anyone's response. But the important point is that you do not have to like someone in order to gain through trade with him. It is not necessary, for example, that we love the milkman, admire the butcher, and revere the candlestick maker for us to find it advantageous to deal with them. Similarly, they may bear us no great love and yet find it profitable to deal with us.

In the case of an unfriendly power, of course, there are additional considerations, many of which can only be alluded to here. The fact is, however, that unlike the milkman, the butcher and the candlestick maker, Cuba has been considered a threat to U.S. security, and we do not wish to help a potential adversary to wreak havoc upon us. The question is still open, however, as to whether trade would be advantageous to us *on balance*. With these thoughts in mind, the following ranking seems to be appropriate. You will notice that not every item has a particular rank order.

1. "Permitted," although this is a pretty unconstrained thing, difficult perhaps to square with the needs of national security.

What Economics is Not 63

2. "Permitted when such exports are part of deals by which we get something we need from Cuba." The trouble with this one is that it might allow us to get sugar that we need badly for consumers, while giving to Cuba jet engines which she needed to increase her war-making potential.
3. "Stopped except in materials which Cuba can acquire from other nations."
4. "Stopped except for nonstrategic (nonwar-making) materials."
5. "Governed by military policy, not economic policy." This phrase suggests a division between these two policies which is difficult to imagine. To strengthen an economy is to strengthen its military position. This difficulty of distinction is perhaps the major objection to this choice.
6. "Stopped." Stopping trade without any qualification is to miss any opportunity to realize gains from trade, even when such opportunities might be of far greater value to the United States than to Cuba. There are, of course, other reasons for preferring any of these choices, but we are looking exclusively at an economic ordering.

The reader may be as surprsied as I was at the pattern of responses to this complicated question. As shown below, there was great clustering in the largest percentage figures.

The most frequent rank assigned to trade policy indicated by the word "stopped" is 6 (last place); 81 percent of the economists assigned this rank. There was a tie for first choice and no fifth choice. Contradiction of my ranking occurs in the choice "governed by military policy, not economic policy" which economists placed first and I placed fifth.

I believe the answers reveal a hint of free-trade bias among most of us.

To emphasize the pattern it may be added here that a random series of replies would show only one-sixth or 16⅔ percent of the replies accorded any given rank.

Rank Order	Percentage of Responses	
1.	50	Permitted.
1.	37	Governed by military policy, not economic policy.
2.	52	Permitted when such exports are part of deals by which we get something we need from Cuba.

64   WHAT IS ECONOMICS?

Rank Order	Percentage of Responses	
3.	37	Stopped except for nonstrategic (non-war-making) materials.
4.	41	Stopped except in materials which Cuba can acquire from other nations.
6.	81	Stopped.

THE TOPICS DEALT WITH IN TEXTBOOKS

A second definition of economics stems from what might be thought of as the table of contents of a typical college textbook. This might be called a topical definition of economics and means that economics is its applications—international trade, labor problems, money and banking, business cycles, organization of industry, growth of developing nations, accounting, managerial practice, and so on, ad infinitum.

A variant of this crude view is an even grosser misconception that looks upon the discipline as the study of even more specific things. Here we find economics misconstrued as the study of the specialization of labor, gold, paper money, wage rates, the quality of merchandise, the Taft-Hartley Act, writing a check, mailing a letter, and so on and on and on. It is as if we were to say that architecture is bridges and sewer pipes, and dentistry is cavities and toothpaste.

As the general discussion of the preceding chapter has shown, economics is not its applications. Rather, economics is one of the special points of view from which insights on human behavior can be meaningfully organized. The principles of this organization are independent of whether that behavior is manifested by nations, labor unions, banks, or other organizations that are of topical interest.

Consider the topic, international trade. What is trade more more than the study of the implications—causes and consequences—of regional specialization among nations and of such institutions as the International Monetary Fund, the World Bank, and others? Trade is the study of the implications of scarcity shown in the relationships among nations.

Trade and other topics are important for study. An economist who knew nothing about trade (or business cycles or industrial structure) is like a lawyer ignorant of torts. Each will, on occasion, suffer in embarrassed silence when the conversation turns toward his empty briefcase. But both are still professionals, economist and lawyer, respectively, whether or not they know particular applications of their crafts. None of this means, of course, that certain applications of economics are not ideal vehicles for teaching and learning the subject.

There is an important change under way that promises to weaken the notion that economics is its applications. College professors, chafing at the massive encyclopedias that are today's textbooks, are turning to responsive publishers who are putting forth single, short, paperback volumes devoted to specific applications. In this way, it is no longer necessary for a college instructor in beginning courses in economics to pretend acquaintance with the thirty-ninth through forty-fifth chapters of the average textbook, which chapters require that he discuss fascism, communism, socialism, developmentalism, and all kinds of currently fashionable topics like the deficit in the balance of payments, the gold flow, and the latest negotiation in the automobile industry. Moreover, as economists come to work more closely with school systems, they are finding that in the public schools, particularly at the lower grade levels, it is both superfluous and misleading to attempt to encompass within a discussion of economics those topics which are largely the outgrowth of momentous changes in social organization since World War II. At the elementary grades, one must deal with the basic elements of economics, and it is a good idea not to stray far from these elements even in secondary schools.

Here we conclude that economics is not its topics.

APPLIED MATHEMATICS

A third erroneous definition of economics that holds dangerous sway among practitioners of the science is that economics is a branch of applied mathematics. This notion is deceptively appealing because of the brilliant results, rigorously demonstrated, in the application of mathematics to particular economic problems. Besides, many important theorems of economics can only be succinctly stated in mathematical terms.

But this erroneous drift of the discipline is really a confusion of techniques with larger systematic thinking. The error flourishes because the vast majority of economists have suffered from so great an ignorance of mathematics that they have no way of arguing against those who speak the alien tongue, those whose troops apparently have conquered so great a domain. Fortunately, economists are becoming increasingly sophisticated in mathematics and, therefore, we may expect that they will be better prepared to defend their traditional bastions. Furthermore, economists with training in mathematics have recognized right along that mathematics and economics are different.*

Not all of the hammering we hear nowadays comes from economists who are building bigger and bigger mathematical matrices. A good deal of the banging is from the valiant efforts of those who got boxed in trying to smash their way out.

Any discipline whose significant relationships may be expressed mathematically is subject to fruitful manipulation in mathematical terms. The serious student of economics will neglect algebra at his peril. But economics is not the algebraic formulation of amenable relationships. It is larger than that, as argued earlier. I can only hope that the nonmathematical writing in these pages supports this conclusion that economics is not applied mathematics.

OBJECTIVES SERVED BY AN ECONOMIC SYSTEM

A fourth view, never explicitly put forward but nevertheless implicitly capturing the imagination of many followers of economics is that the science is essentially a study of particular objectives. These objectives typically are those upon which there

---

* See below, pp. 115 to 117. Unfortunately, the youngest generation of economists is making such a good living out of stochastic processes that they are little inclined to study economics. Their writings and research, subsidized by government and philanthropy, promise us untold years of computerized spectacles.

is a wide political consensus and whose content is often largely defined in terms of economic causes and consequences. To state some of the objectives is to see their appeal. They include economic growth, economic security, economic freedom, economic stability, and economic justice.

Like the topics approach but more insidious because of its greater appeal, this definition of economics in terms of goals has exerted noticeable influence. It is, of course, clearly at variance with earlier discussions in this book. Its inadequacy comes to the fore if we consider that these goals are simply highly valued aims of society but that it takes more than the implications of desirable objectives to make a science. To determine their adequacy, moreover, what if patriotism, military preparedness, better education, and mother love were added to the five enumerated goals? Who would dissent from their inclusion? Yet how would these square with a definition of the subject? The fact is that the multiplicity of human ends precludes any such organization of economic thinking and, in any case, the approach is wrong in principle.

The approach is wrong in principle because objectives have no absolute definition in economics; they have meaning chiefly in relation to the resources, productive processes, outputs, and consumption processes that are along the path to their achievement. Nor are they inclusive enough of the aims of a pluralistic society. And, finally, they have little or no use in such mundane but important problems at the microeconomic level as how to end the pollution of a city's harbor or whether a firm can afford to pay a wage increase to its employees.

None of this is an attack on the objectives listed above, nor is it an excuse for eliminating the discussion of public policy in these matters or for refusing to recognize the great value to learning and to teaching that such discussion may provide. Economics has much to contribute to the achievement of society's objectives, and students of economics should be introduced to the subject through applications that explicitly deal with major objectives. This is a far cry, however, from attempting to force all of economic thinking into five boxes that happen at the moment to be central goals laden with economic content. We therefore conclude that economics is not objectives.

GENERAL PROBLEM SOLVING

One of the most rewarding methods of teaching and learning is instruction that involves problem solving. In applying his knowledge to a concrete problem, the student simulates most of the conditions that face a professional practitioner. The hope of solution can be a mighty stimulus to learning. For these reasons, both the natural and the social sciences have come to rely heavily upon carefully selected problems to promote effective education.

With increasing emphasis upon problem solving, however, a danger has arisen that economics might become virtually synonymous with this method. While no one can take exception to this if he is free to define problem solving to suit his fancy, it is equally obvious that problem solving can be made the definition of chemistry, biology, tax accountancy, or any other field of study. There is nothing peculiar about economics in relation to the solution of problems.

To illustrate economics as rubrics, we may state a general format for problem solving in the social sciences. One incantation might go something like this:

Identify the problem.
Gather the facts about the problem.
Study the facts.
Analyze the alternative solutions to the problem.
Introduce the values or criteria which an acceptable solution must satisfy.
Determine which alternative solution best satisfies the values.
(Do not pass "Go"; do not collect one hundred dollars.)
Pick the best solution.

Now, what is wrong with this procedure (aside from the parenthetical expression, of course)? There is nothing wrong with it as such, but clearly, the procedure has nothing *special* to do with economics. Or with paleontology. Or with etiology. The procedure is indifferent to disciplines and vice versa.

It follows, therefore, that the crucial matter of understanding the nature of economics is not aided by a helpful method of solving problems in general. Therefore, economics is not general problem solving.

QUESTIONS

A QUESTION OF RECOGNIZING PROCESSES CONFORMING TO THE STRUCTURE OF ECONOMICS

Which one of the following processes most nearly resembles an economic process, that is, a process described in economic terms? Circle the letter of the answer you choose.

    a. Slicing of meat in an automatic meat-slicing machine.
    b. A satellite orbiting in space.
    c. Taking a multiple-choice examination in biology.
    d. Traveling by airplane from New York to San Francisco.

ANSWERS

A QUESTION OF RECOGNIZING PROCESSES CONFORMING TO THE STRUCTURE OF ECONOMICS

The best answer here seems to be c, "taking a multiple choice examination in biology." Each of the answers, of course, has some connection with things economic; and some of the wrong answers appear to have more connection than this correct one. That is, meat and slicing machines, satellites, and airplanes and travel are all things that have a potential economic dimension to them. The emphasis in this choice, however, is on *processes*: slicing, orbiting, taking, travelling. There is little that is economic in the automatic slicing of meat (however much analysis there might be in the production process of the meat industry or the slicing machine industry). The same may be said of a satellite orbiting in space: it is of no more interest to economists than the obiting moon, the asteroids, and the comets. These are of interest to astrophysicists and astronomers. Similarly, travelling by airplane across the country conjures up the joys of air travel, the good meals, the comfortable seats, the movies and stereophonic tapes that are sometimes provided for the comfort of passengers. But there is little that is obviously economic.

The taking of a multiple choice examination in biology (or any subject) has in it all the ingredients of an economic problem. Indeed, elsewhere in these pages the analogy has been drawn between the allocation of a student's time among subjects in order to "maximize" his grade average and the process of resource allocation as understood by economists. *Taking* an examination where one must allocate time among questions in order that additional minutes are spent only on questions that may raise (maximize) one's achievement—this is a process closely analogous to economic processes.

A preponderant percentage of economists chose answer c as shown in the following distribution:

   a. 13
   b. 16
   c. 61
   d. 10

OTHER MISCONCEPTIONS

There are several other misconceptions about economics that have done much mischief to the understanding of the subject. While these are not well organized into large explanations like those erroneous views dealt with in the preceding five sections of this chapter, they are sufficiently widespread and damaging to command our attention.

The first misconception is that economic analysis rests upon an assumption that human wants are "unlimited." We often read statements of the central economic problem that run like this: the economic problem is characterized by man's attempts to satisfy his unlimited wants through the allocation of scarce resources.

About such a statement we should ask, What is meant by the words "unlimited wants?" Does it mean that a person or a group of people can have wants that are unlimited *in number*? Or does it mean that the wants are unlimited in the sense that (whether limited or unlimited in number) some of them defy attempts to

What Economics is Not 71

satisfy them? Or does it mean both things, that is, man has an unlimited *number* of wants and some of them are *insatiable*?

We may then ask ourselves: Do I have an unlimited number of wants? Do I have a single want that defies satisfaction? Do I know anyone who suffers in either of these two ways?

I have heard it said in defense of the idea of "unlimited wants" that it was never meant to apply to an individual. For no single person, it is said, can have a want that cannot be satisfied nor an unlimited number of wants. But, it is argued, for the whole of society there are unlimited wants. This argument is illogical. As long as society consists of a limited number of people whose wants are also limited, no summation or aggregation will yield an unlimited total. The sum of a finite number of things is a finite sum.

These questions are of great importance to an understanding of the nature of economics and of its practical application to specific problems. Just consider how difficult it is to imagine trying to solve problems that involve wants that are unlimited—infinite—either in number or in their demands for satisfaction. The plight of the consumer is indeed pitiable if he suffers from so voracious an appetite. And how is he to proceed rationally to allocate his resources among his infinite wants?*

There is another difficulty with the spurious notion of unlimited wants, and this is the suggestion that the reason resources are *scarce* is that wants are *unlimited*. The idea here is that resources are only scarce in relation to the wants they serve to satisfy. Therefore, if wants are unlimited, resources must be scarce in relation to them.

Now, it is true that the economic scarcity of resources only makes sense in relation to the wants they satisfy. And "fewness" has nothing to do with economic scarcity. As economists have

---

* The mathematically inclined reader will see that we have here a problem that nearly defies solution. In principle, of course, an infinite number of wants can be rank-ordered by their importance where importance is defined as the amount of satisfaction derived from the allocation of some standard resource unit toward gratification. Then the problem of maximizing satisfaction becomes manageable. Whether this mathematical "solution" has any bearing on consumer behavior is another matter.

long pointed out, there are fewer rotten eggs than fresh eggs but it is the fresh ones that are economically scarce, that is, command a price. This is because, of course, there is a want or demand for the fresh eggs and none for the rotten eggs. But does any of this require that any want or any number of wants be assumed unlimited? The answer must be, no. A commodity is scarce because it commands a price, not because there is an unlimited want for it.

There is another point to be made about the doubtful concept of unlimited wants. Economists are rightfully anxious to emphasize that their analysis is applicable to virtually all societies of whatever time or place. The church of today, the city-state of ancient Greece, the culture of prehistoric man—all of these have economic aspects to them. All can, in a measure, be better understood through the application of economic analysis. Yet are we to believe that all societies are characterized by people of unlimited wants? The monasteries of today and yesterday? The feudal manor of medieval times? The aborigines of Australia? The Sioux and Cherokees? To express the idea of all people being subjected to unlimited wants is to be repelled by it. Therefore, economists cannot take the (correct) position that economic analysis is widely applicable to societies of all times and places and, at the same time, contend that such analysis requires an assumption about the boundlessness of human wants. Many societies to which the economist would direct his analysis have not exhibited any such condition.

Then, what is to be done? Is economic analysis inapplicable to peoples of limited appetites? Or is the assumption of such appetites untenable? From everything that has been said to this point, the answer is clear: the assumption of unlimited wants is untenable. It must go. It is probably a false assumption. Its validity cannot, in any case, be demonstrated. And finally, why should economics be saddled with an unnecessary assumption of questionable validity? Of course, it should not.

We need not spend any time examining the consequences of dropping an unnecessary assumption from economic analysis. There simply are no consequences to analysis. But it may be worthwhile to ask how the assumption got onto the stage in the first place. I should guess that it entered current discussion because the *appearance* in Western, industrialized nations of consumer markets is an *appearance* of unlimited appetites. Particularly in contrast to less economically developed areas of the world, the consumer appears insatiable. And some economists have made this appearance an article of economic faith. (What a belief in unlimited wants does to any notion of progress—the progressive satisfaction of wants—is a horrible thing to contemplate.)

A secondary explanation for adherence to a belief in unlimited wants has to do with the dominant ideology of Western, free enterprise economies. If wants are unlimited and if this is the motive force behind economic aspiration and achievement, then this force is unlimited too. Therefore, the propulsion upward and upward of Western economies is assured. But this is nothing other than bad philosophical presupposition. It is roughly on a par with a crude, Marxian, "materialistic" interpretation of history. And, as earlier mentioned, speculation about whether finite creatures can be seized by infinite wants is fruitless and unnecessary speculation for the social scientist.

What proponents of the idea of unlimited wants probably mean might be something like this: man typically wants more of some things than he has and this condition of wanting has persisted throughout much of recorded history. This, indeed, is a reasonable proposition. However, whether even this moderate proposition has anything essential to do with economic analysis is open to question.*

A second misconception about economics is that the subject matter is chiefly occupied with the production and consumption of things that contribute to society's "material welfare" or that influence "material well-being" or "material standards of living."

Current emphasis upon this notion of "material" is curious. The notion that economics is peculiarly concerned with material

---

* Perhaps some people confuse wants with mere imaginings. They may think that man's imagination is unlimited (another nondemonstrable and unnecessary idea), and therefore he can imagine wanting things without limit. But is man's imagination not his greatest resource? If it is, then his resources are unlimited—or at least as unlimited as his wants. I owe this interesting idea to John Lawrence.

welfare was exploded by Lionel Robbins more than thirty years ago.* Yet since this strange idea refuses to die, let us examine its meaning.

Economics does, indeed, deal with material things both as outputs (houses, bridges, radios) and as resources or inputs (steam shovels, land, laborers). This might seem to lend to the subject matter of the science a peculiarly material cast; but even a superficial examination of these material things reveals that it is not their physical manifestation that is important. Rather, it is the *services* they render. It is the services of houses, bridges, and radios that consumers want. It is the services of steam shovels, land, and laborers that business firms want. And there is nothing material about these services. Let engineering have the nature of the physical world; economics studies relationships, and the relationships are primarily among services. Most of the matters with which economics is occupied do not manifest an obviously close connection to things material: the satisfaction of consumers' wants, the transformation of resources into outputs, the weighing of alternative advantages, and so forth.

If we were to offer an explanation of the tenacity of this perverse doctrine of materiality, we should simply say that, just as psychology appears to deal with the mind and theology with the soul, so economics appears to deal with the belly, the seat of those "unlimited" wants that were exorcised in preceding pages. Philosophers like Carlyle are encouraged to apply to economics the epithet, "pig philosophy," yet no one who has thought deeply about the science or who has read the works of any economist who has thought deeply about it will promote so foolish a view.

Consideration of the inappropriateness of emphasis upon the material side of human behavior (whatever that may mean) forms a natural link to our discussion of a final misconception. This we may call the "vagaries of economic goals."

While it is sometimes useful to speak of "economic" goals, we must be very careful in doing so. This is because goals themselves are usually not amenable to economic analysis; it is rather the

---

* *Op. cit.*, pp. 4-11. Robbins carefully explains how this misconception has flourished even among eminent economists. The reader, who remains unconvinced by the few paragraphs presented above, may be persuaded by Robbins' argument.

application of the means to their attainment that is subject to analysis.* Thus, for example, the choice of the kind of temple for the worship of God is not well suited to economic analysis. But the choices of stone and mortar for a cathedral along with other considerations of cost do fall squarely within the province of economic analysis. There is a production function in church building. Consequently, not the ends or objectives of human activity are the subjects of economic inquiry but rather the relationships of those ends to the scarce resources used in their attainment.

There is no need to avoid the common practice of calling economic goals those goals whose pursuit is especially laden with economic consequence, or those goals that are paramount in most public discussions of economic policy. But, as pointed out earlier, one should avoid organizing the discipline itself about any particular set of goals. And one should avoid the misconception that economic analysis is suited to the evaluation of societal goals. Economics can pronounce on the cost of attaining one goal in terms of the attainment of others. But it cannot weigh and rank the goals or objectives themselves; it contains no ostensible ethical or esthetic criteria for making such judgments of value.

---

* Cf. Robbins, *Op. cit.*, pp. 24ff.

CHAPTER

6

Free Light Bulbs?

THE two preceding chapters have sketched with a few broad strokes what economics is and what it is not. Now, if the sketch is of any use, we should see whether or not a problem in economic analysis can in fact be understood in the terms that have been set forth. In this chapter, a test is made of the framework by applying it to a specific case. While it is too much to hope that everything earlier mentioned will find a place in this exposition, it may fairly be expected that there will be a smiling congruence between the face of economics and the image of the particular problem we have chosen to analyze.

Our problem comes to us from a practice of an electric utility in Michigan, the Detroit Edison Company. In the area it serves, the Company supplies residents with new light bulbs in exchange for burnt-out bulbs that are brought to the Company's local offices. In addition, the Company makes certain repairs to electrical appliances at no charge. The new light bulbs and the repairs, we may assume, are consistent with the utility's hope that homes will be well lighted, appliances will hum, and consumers will use many kilowatt-hours of electricity.

The policy of providing light bulbs gives us the title of the present chapter, "Free Light Bulbs?" The deliberate use of the question mark suggests something about the problem. Are the light bulbs supplied by the utility to its customers really free? Of course, it is obvious that the bulbs cost somebody some money: light bulbs do not grow on trees; they are not gifts of nature. The question is, Who pays for them? And how much?

I first wondered about this, when, for over three years, I had the good fortune to live in the Detroit area. However, it was not until my attention was brought to a specific interpretation of the Company's policy that I gave it serious thought. As it turned out, a colleague on the faculty of Oakland University, an historian, had told some members of his class that the reason Detroit Edison was able to supply free light bulbs to its customers was a bequest by Thomas A. Edison. In his will, it was reported, Edison had left a sum of money to be used to buy light bulbs for customers in the Detroit area.

While I should not want to suggest that this explanation of the company's policy is typical of the fruits of historical research, it does inform us symbolically of one kind of thinking. My historian friend apparently saw no logical argument why it was extremely unlikely that free light bulbs were being provided as the result of historical legacy. To an economist, however, the idea seems patently absurd. In the first place, Edison died so many years ago (1931) that for him to have been able to bequeath a sum of money large enough to meet the needs of the increasing population of the Detroit area and the increasing use of electricity per person was most unlikely. The costs of such an operation would be enormous, as we shall later see. In addition, it seems a strange use for a bequest, no matter how much allowance is made for the humanitarian motives that prompt philanthropy.

As I shall show in a note at the end of this chapter, an inquiry addressed to the Detroit Edison Company provided an estimate of the cost of this service and also laid to rest the peculiar ghost of Thomas Edison's generosity.

Before throwing the switch of our analytic powers in connection with the problem at hand, we may first say something about the deceptively simple appearance of this kind of problem. The matter of finding out who pays for something often appears to be an easy matter yet, in fact, it is extremely tricky. Sometimes we unwittingly accept superficial explanations that appeal to common sense but that, on closer scrutiny, are found to be wholly without merit.

As a ridiculous example of superficial explanation, imagine someone's suggesting that the people who pay the social security taxes levied on employers' payrolls are the mailmen who deliver the checks to the U.S. Treasury! This is obvious foolishness: the mailmen merely transmit the payments. Equally foolish would be the suggestion that the bookkeepers who make out their employers' checks are the ones who pay the tax. We know that the sums of money involved do not come out of the funds of either bookkeepers or mailmen.

At a deeper level of analysis we might entertain the notion that the social security taxes are paid for by the employers of labor: it is against their bank balances, as a matter of fact, that checks are drawn to the order of the U.S. Treasury. But then we may recall that half of the tax is a deduction from the wages of employees and the other half is "paid" by the employers. Would we be right in saying that employers pay half and employees pay half? Our answer must be, probably not. In most instances, employees are paying most of the tax.

How does economic analysis arrive at the conclusion that employees are paying most of the social security tax on payrolls? It is simply that a tax on wages of, say, 6 percent is just like a rise in wages of that same percentage *as seen by the employer*. Instead of paying a worker $2 an hour, he now pays $2.12, even though the U.S. Treasury gets the $.12, not the worker. Therefore, the $.12 is, in a real sense, a form of wages foregone. If the tax had not been imposed, the wage of the employed worker could have been that much higher. There would have been no difference in the employer's wage costs whether he paid the worker or the Treasury. So, no matter who writes the check, no matter who nominally makes payment, the real cost is borne by those who have less than they otherwise would have had.*

---

* As we shall soon see in dealing with "free" light bulbs, it is likely in most cases that real costs are widely shared. In the illustration of social security taxes, we neglect this sharing for convenience of exposition.

Two other points must also be made. (1) The fact that, upon retirement,

LIGHT BULBS

Having taken a quick look at an economic approach to assigning costs, we now return to the light bulb problem and set down the few facts we have at hand. The Detroit Edison Company states that, on average, the bulbs cost the Company $.13 apiece (in 1962). By contrast, if customers had bought the bulbs in retail stores, the cost to them would have averaged $.25. Again the question, Who pays for the bulbs?

As a first approximation, one can suggest that it must be the consumers of electric power who pay for the bulbs. Virtually all of the money the company receives comes from consumers of power, and it is clear the bulbs are purchased out of the revenues the company thus receives. It would seem probable then that the light bulbs are purchased by the utility out of the money the utility receives from the customers.

A closer examination suggests that this answer may be quite superficial; it is possible that some other recipient of income from the company receives a smaller payment because funds are expended for the purchase of bulbs. Following this line of reasoning, it might be that profits are lower than they otherwise would be; perhaps wages are lower or materials purchases or rent or interest paid on bonded indebtedness. Thus, to state the issue in its most general terms, there are two possibilities: consumers of power are paying for the bulbs in the form of higher prices for

---

workers will receive benefits from the social security system in no way affects our analysis of who is *now* paying the costs. Especially when payments from and benefits to a worker are separate in time, we must treat each as analytically distinct. After all, it is the workers who are *now* retired who are now receiving benefits from current tax collections. And they are making no payments into the system. (2) The costs of any practice take a wide variety of forms, not many of which can be dealt with in these pages. For example, social security taxes may have such side effects as burdening business with fears about the welfare state and creating financial drives among political groups who wish to lobby against the social security system. All of this may lead to new costs borne by diverse individuals. But these costs, real and important though they may be, cannot be handled here.

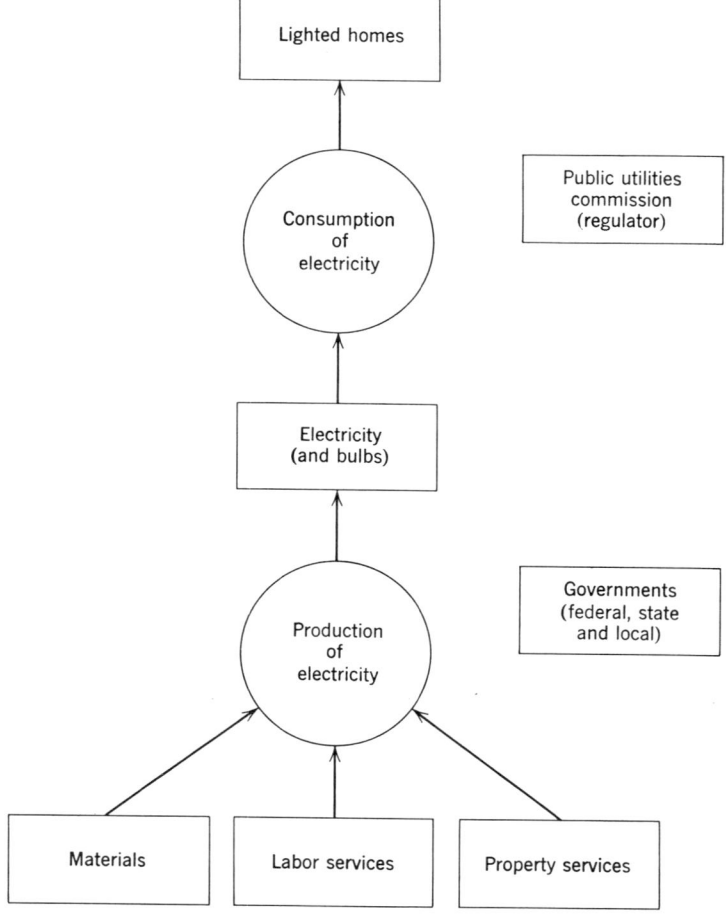

Fig. 6.1 A scheme for examining the question of "free" light bulbs.

electricity which reflect this additional cost or other claimants to the company's revenues are receiving less as a result of this policy. Obviously, there can well be some combination of these two general explanations.

Figure 6.1 shows the components of the problem. You will notice that it is constructed like earlier diagrams that depicted economic activity in five parts. Reading from the top, we notice that the objective served by this system is lighted homes. (We neglect the other uses of electricity for purposes of this analysis.) Immediately below, we see the consumption circle which shows that it is the consumption of electricity that enables consumers to achieve the objective of the system. In the box below consumption, we see the output of the system which is kilowatt hours of electricity. In this special case, we have another commodity which is noted in parentheses, namely, the light bulbs which are the focus of our attention. The light bulbs, of course, enter into the system even though they are not produced by the electric utility.

Below the output box we see the circle of production indicating the generation of electricity. This is meant to symbolize the productive process of combining resources according to certain technological and price relationships among the factors of production. The factors of production themselves, the resources going into the production of electricity, are noted in the three boxes at the bottom of the diagram. Here we show, from left to right, the materials that are supplied to this company, principally coal for generating electricity, light bulbs that are purchased from various suppliers, and other kinds of things like paper for the secretaries to type replies to inquiring professors, paper clips, and so forth. In the second box, we see the supply of labor that comes from workers employed by the company. Labor services, of course, include the labor of the managerial staff as well as that of workers directly engaged in production. And finally, we see the property used by the utility. Most property is owned by stockholders who receive a share of profits for its use. The services of this property—the land, the plant, the equipment—all contribute to the generation of electricity. Not shown separately in the diagram are the services of property owned by others. For example, if land or equipment is rented by the utility, then rental payments are made to owners of such property.

The Public Utility Commission is shown as a regulator of the whole system. In the case of a public utility, the Commission has the regulatory function of insuring that, in return for a monopoly franchise, the company renders good service to consumers at reasonable prices. In determining what reasonable prices are, the Commission must make allowance for the necessary costs incurred by the company, including the profits earned by stockholders on their investment. As we shall see, a knowledge of this institutional arrangement and the laws under which it operates is important to answering questions like the one we are investigating.

In another box we have represented the place of federal, state, and local governments. The reason for citing governments is that they, too, have a stake in the revenues of the utility. The federal and state governments levy a tax on the income of the utility, and local government places a tax upon the property.

We may now briefly restate our problem in more precise terms and then list succinctly the various explanations, realizing that any one or a combination of those groups listed may be bearing the cost.

The problem of who is paying for the light bulbs may be rephrased in the following fashion. If the policy were now abandoned, what group would then have to bear these costs and what group, if any, would be relieved of these costs? We must refer to both the bearing and relieving of costs since we want to arrive at the net position of the many participants in the system. Thus, we see that the cost of a policy is the same as the gain (or loss) that would be experienced by participants if the policy were not followed.

1. Hypothesis: Consumers are paying for the light bulbs. If the policy were not in effect, the charges for electricity would fall. (But, of course, consumers would incur a new expense in having to buy their bulbs.)

2. Hypothesis: Stockholders are paying for the light bulbs. If the policy were abandoned, profits earned by the utility would be increased.

3. Hypothesis: Workers are paying for the light bulbs. If the policy were abandoned, wages and salaries would rise.

4. Hypothesis: Materials suppliers are paying for the bulbs. If the policy were discontinued, suppliers would receive larger payments.

5. The fifth point will only become clearer in subsequent discussion. Here we may suggest the hypothesis that certain other

businesses are paying for the light bulbs. If the policy were abandoned, their receipts would rise.

6. Hypothesis: Governments are paying for the bulbs. If the policy were not followed, tax collections would increase. (Of course, by the phrase "governments are paying" we mean that those who pay taxes to governments are bearing the costs.)

The convenience of the diagram on p. 80 is apparent from these hypotheses. Thus, referring to that diagram, we locate consumers at the top, those who enjoy the lighted homes; they are the group of our number 1 hypothesis. Stockholders are at the bottom right and are the subject of number 2 hypothesis. Workers, at bottom center, are featured in number 3 hypothesis, and materials suppliers at bottom left are included in number 4 hypothesis. Other firms, the group in number 5 hypothesis, are not shown in the diagram but may be considered fivefold activities just like the utility. Governments are a separate box in the sketch, and they are the actors in number 6 hypothesis. We may emphasize, again, the generality of our scheme for problem solving in economics.

But we should go farther than merely saying that the diagram *locates* most of those groups at whose behavior one should look in assessing the impact of economic policy. When the *relationships* among the participants are examined, when the components are viewed as integral parts of an operating *system*, then analysis is possible. Especially important are assumed characteristics of behavior such as the maximizing of profits by the firm and "getting the most satisfaction for their money" by consumers.

We now take up each of the five hypotheses about who is helped and who is hurt by the free light bulb policy.

1. *Consumers.* The cost to the utility of buying and handling the bulbs it provides its customers is part of the regular cost of doing business. The propriety of this cost is recognized by the regulatory authority. Therefore, the rates charged for electricity reflect, in whole or in part, this cost. We note provisionally that consumers are likely candidates for carrying the load.

We must add immediately that the *net* cost to consumers must be close to zero or even negative. This is because if the policy were abandoned, the decline they would experience in their electric bills would presumably be more than offset by a near doubling of the cost of their purchasing bulbs at retail. You will recall that the company pays an average cost of $.13 for bulbs which sell at retail for $.25.

In slight mitigation of the effect of a rise to the $.25 retail price of bulbs is another effect opposite in direction. For if the provision of bulbs has stimulated the consumption of electricity, then abandoning the policy will mean a decline in consumption. Therefore, without the policy, consumers would need fewer light bulbs and so they would not have to spend on bulbs the "twice as much" implied by a near doubling of the price of bulbs. There is, however, a force working opposite to this. If the utility has been able to produce electricity at lower cost because of larger consumption stimulated by this policy, then, under the present policy, consumers are benefiting from what we may call the economies of large-scale production. What this means is that the average cost of producing electricity would be higher if consumption were below its present level because of this lack of stimulation. As economists generally would argue, an industry like a public utility that has very large fixed costs of operation (the costs of the generating equipment, the transmission lines), costs which are large in relation to the labor and other variable costs, usually does operate under circumstances of declining average cost. Therefore, it is likely that costs of production are, on the average, lower at higher levels of output.*

---

* A somewhat more rigorous statement of this matter can be phrased in terms of marginal cost. That is, the extra costs of generating another few thousand kilowatt hours of electricity, provided the installation has the capacity, are usually quite low. Here is an instance of studying the costs at the margin like that encountered in earlier pages when the question of the student's allocation of time between mathematics and literature was discussed.

A clearer example of this kind of low, extra cost can be drawn from the railroad industry. For example, what is the extra cost of hauling a passenger from New York to Chicago on a railroad train if you maintain a regular schedule of such trains and there is space available on the train to accommodate a passenger? Obviously, the extra cost that a railroad would encounter is very, very small. It would hardly be noticeable in the fuel bill of the diesel locomotive or on the wear and tear of the tracks to haul another person this distance. On the other hand, the total cost of the operation of running a train over this distance, no matter how you calculate it, is very

As a minor point in this connection, it should be noted that by escaping from the ordinary pricing system, that is, in not buying their bulbs on the market, consumers of electricity are engaged in what may be called a kind of internal subsidy. That is, those consumers who do not use very much electricity and who are careful about not breaking light bulbs may in fact be subsidizing those consumers who use a lot of electricity and who may be careless in smashing light bulbs. It is much like life insurance, where it is those who survive who pay the benefits to those who don't survive. So also, in this case, those who are wasteful in their use of these bulbs for which they are not directly charged are subsidized by those who are conservative in their use of this non-priced commodity.

2. *Stockholders.* We should next consider whether it is the stockholders in the company (whose profits may be lower) who are paying the cost of light bulbs. The logic here is straightforward. If the company did not buy bulbs, its costs of operations would drop and its profits would rise—neglecting the effects of the policy in stimulating the consumption of electricity.

There are several reasons for believing that this cost does not come out of profits. In the first place, the policy would not be adopted by a management intent upon earning a good return for their stockholders if the stockholders are to be saddled with this extra cost. Second, as we briefly noted earlier, the Public Service Commission which regulates the rates charged consumers also pays attention to a "fair rate of return," that is, the profit rate to be earned by stockholders in the regulated utility (usually a six percent rate of return on invested capital is considered fair). We note furthermore that the costs of the bulbs are a legitimate cost of production which the Public Service Commission will allow in calculating the rate of profit. This is consistent with the hypothesis that stockholders are not bearing the burden. Moreover, in calculating a rate of return it is suggested that the cost of the inventory of light bulbs is a fair part of the rate base. (See the second paragraph in the letter at the end of this chapter.)

With respect to the stockholders, then, we may conclude that

---

high. This is another way of pointing out the fact that there are economies of scale in the production of those goods and services in which a relatively large capital investment is necessary.

sound management would repudiate the policy if it impaired the profits earned by the company and, second, that the costs incurred are allowable by the Public Service Commission before the calculation of profits. Therefore, it is unlikely that these costs are being met from stockholders' earnings.

3. *Workers.* We shall deal only briefly with the hypothesis that the cost of the bulbs is being borne by workers whose wages would otherwise be higher. Since labor is a mobile factor of production and workers have the alternative of leaving this industry if wages are below what is paid in comparable employments elsewhere, it seems highly unlikely that there could be a lower wage because of the policy. (If labor were a good substitute for light bulbs in production, a different inference would be drawn. Compare the present case with that of barber shops that gave their customers a tonic that would slow the growth of hair.)

4. *Materials suppliers.* Are the suppliers of materials contributing to the cost of the bulbs? It seems unnecessary to treat suppliers of all materials to the utility in answering this question. However, there is one group of suppliers who deserve special attention, namely, the manufacturers of the light bulbs. It seems possible that the utility may be able to make them sell bulbs at a lower cost than would otherwise prevail and that they, therefore, are bearing some of the cost of this policy; in its absence they would be receiving a higher price for their product. We have already noted that the average retail price is nearly twice as high as the price paid by the utility for bulbs.

It must be emphasized that we are *not* saying that bulb suppliers are helping to finance any of the average company cost of $.13 a bulb. Rather, we say that without this policy bulbs might sell for a higher price, some of which price is now lost to the suppliers.

The kind of case we have in mind here is known to economists as "monopsony," that is, a market in which a large purchaser of a certain resource may be able to compel the suppliers of that resource to accept less in payment than would be paid if the buyer were not so large a purchaser. Put more bluntly, a large purchaser has some bargaining power in dickering with the suppliers who are dependent, to a great extent, on the firm's purchases.

This is a clear possibility. Yet it must be pointed out at once that the price received by suppliers (such as General Electric, Westinghouse, Sylvania, and others) is not nearly so low as it might first appear. Obviously, the utility buys its bulbs at a kind of wholesale price which may be exactly the same as would be paid by any hardware store, grocery, or appliance store that bought bulbs. Thus, we must avoid assuming that the suppliers would receive the price of $.25 that consumers would have to pay in the absence of this policy instead of the $.13 that the company pays on average for the bulbs it buys. All we can say at this point is that there is no evidence contained in the little information we have to support the notion that the suppliers of bulbs are bearing some of the costs.

5. *Other firms.* Is it other firms who are bearing some of the cost of this policy? Having just noticed the "spread" between the price paid by the utility and the one the consumers would have to pay—the difference between $.13 and $.25—we raise the very important possibility that there is a cost borne by potential storekeepers and their employees who would be selling light bulbs to consumers if the utility had not largely preempted this field. Thus, we may safely assume that if it had not been for the present policy, part of the difference in price would have gone to those appliance and hardware stores who, in other areas of the country, sell light bulbs. If retailers have been able to sell other things in place of bulbs, as is likely, then their share of the burden is not so heavy.

Now, of course, employment in the utility may be assumed to be greater because of the extra workers who are needed to handle, account for, and exchange light bulbs. Therefore, while employment (and profits) in what we may call light bulb stores is slightly lower because they handle many fewer bulbs under the present arrangement, some of this employment is compensated for by employment in the utility. There remains, then, the likelihood that proprietors of those stores who are not getting this business are bearing some of the cost of the present policy. Indeed, we may be fairly certain of this.

6. *Governments.* Finally, we should consider whether the federal government that receives income from the taxation of corporate profits may be bearing some of the costs. While we shall deal here only with the federal (or state) government, the

fact is, of course, that the same reasoning would apply to other governments whose receipts vary with the earnings of corporations.

We may say at the outset that it is unlikely that much of the cost is borne by government. Yet for the sake of a more complete picture, we should consider the implications of the present policy for tax revenues.

At a superficial level of analysis, it may be suggested that if the company didn't incur the expense of buying light bulbs, it would then earn higher profits. If it earned higher profits, the federal government's tax receipts would increase. Therefore, it would appear that the federal government is bearing part of the cost.

However, we noticed earlier that there are two constraints on profits that suggest there is little or no effect upon them from the bulb policy. We said, when discussing the likelihood that stockholders are bearing the burden, that if this were the case then management wouldn't follow the policy. And we added that the regulatory commission must afford stockholders a fair rate of return on invested capital. It follows loosely from this that profits would in fact not be larger in the absence of this policy and therefore federal revenues from taxation of profits would not be larger. We conclude, therefore, that the federal government (and presumably the state government) is not bearing any substantial fraction of the cost of the light bulbs.

We note that the effect upon the revenues of local government which taxes the company's property, but not income, could be substantially different. However, since the inventory of light bulbs is a pretty small item in the valuation of property subject to taxation, it seems unlikely here also that there is much effect upon local government revenues from this policy.

We may conclude that there are two groups that appear to be bearing most of the cost associated with the policy under consideration. First, the consumers who are paying higher prices for electricity and, second, the proprietors of stores that sell light bulbs. While consumers are bearing the cost, we know that it is probably next to nothing if we allow for what they would have to pay if they were compelled to buy bulbs at retail. Proprietors, on the contrary, who derive no direct benefit from the policy suffer a loss of revenue they otherwise would receive.

QUESTIONS

ECONOMIC AND NONECONOMIC

From the following list of different kinds of data, place a check mark in front of those items that are especially economic:

_____ 1. The price of wheat per bushel.
_____ 2. The population of the United States in 1968.
_____ 3. The number of commercial banks in New York State.
_____ 4. Average rainfall over the Mississippi River Basin.
_____ 5. The profits of corporations.
_____ 6. The Constitution of the United States.
_____ 7. An index of the cost of living.
_____ 8. Membership in the Nazi Party in 1923.
_____ 9. *The Economic Report of the President.*
_____ 10. The longing for immortality.

What basis or criterion did you apply in deciding which items were especially economic and which were not?

ANSWERS

ECONOMIC AND NONECONOMIC

The items with odd numbers are the ones that appear to be "especially economic," that is, 1, 3, 5, 7, and 9. And they appear economic because economics commonly deals with prices, banking, profits, indexes of living costs, and economic reporting.

Close consideration, however, suggests a problem. Take item 4, "average rainfall over the Mississippi River Basin." Suppose an economist were trying to explain the prices of wheat, corn, and other agricultural commodities grown in the midwest. If there had been a drought which seriously affected production of these commodities, might he not have to take into account the effect of drought in reducing supplies and raising prices? And might not average rainfall be a good measure of drought conditions? A yes answer poses a question about what is meant by data that are "especially economic."

Similarly, all of the even-numbered items could be considered data representing forces with potentially large economic influence. But something is not to be called "economic" either because it is a cause (like weather) of economic effects; or because it is an effect with economic causes (like suicides resulting from the stock market crash of 1929). The cause-and-effect relationship doesn't help much in deciding what is economic and what is not.

This leads to a powerful, systematic definition of which data are to be classed as economic and which are to be classed noneconomic. We may choose to say that data which are determined (explained) largely by economic analysis are economic; data which are not determined (explained) largely by economic analysis are noneconomic. The latter data may have a lot of economic causes or consequences, but they are classed as noneconomic because economic science isn't of much help in explaining them generally.

By analogy, we may say that an electric lighting system may be part of a class of things called electrical, but the hand (cause) that throws the switch is not. Neither is the body that gets electrocuted (consequence). The principles of electricity do not well explain hands and bodies any more than the principles of economics explain weather and suicides.

Now we may reconsider our initial decision on what items are economic and what are not. I should retain the odd-numbered items except for number 3, "the number of commercial banks in New York State," and maybe number 9, *"The Economic Report of the President."* The number of banks seems to me something more decided by the laws of the State than by anything especially economic; and the President's *Report,* like any book, is not well explained by economics although, of course, much of its contents is. The even-numbered items remain classed as noneconomic except, perhaps, for a follower of the historian, Charles Beard. Such a follower might say that number 6, "the Constitution of the United States," was determined by forces amenable to economic analysis.* (A doctrinaire Marxist would agree and would say the same about all 10 items!)

The point of this exercise is not to show that there are hard and fast lines to be drawn between what is and what is not economic. Indeed, there are instances where no such lines can be drawn. Rather, the point here is to show a reasonable way of classifying things so that they may be better understood and analyzed.

The scientist's way of making this kind of division is to call *endogenous*

---

* Charles Beard, *An Economic Interpretation of the Constitution.*

those things that are explained *within* a system and *exogenous* those that are explained *outside* the system.

This question, unfortunately, was devised too recently to be checked by the group of economists who read other questions.

The case of "free" light bulbs provided by a utility has interesting parallels in many other productive processes. For example, there is the trading stamp practice and its counterparts by which merchants give "free" gifts to customers who save the trading stamps given with purchases. This practice is not unlike that earlier analyzed for the Detroit Edison Company. And indeed, all kinds of "gifts" contingent upon purchases may be analyzed in the same general terms. Usually, it will be found that it is the consumers who are bearing some or all of the costs; that there is an internal subsidy within the group of consumers, that is, some consumers who collect these stamps are subsidized by others who do not. This parallels what we have seen in the light bulb case. It seems least likely that the stockholders of the corporation are bearing the burden but likely that competing enterprises are suffering some of the burden.

It is also worth noting that our analysis sheds some light on the perennial issue of "double taxation." While we have not gone very far in examining the implications of tax policies on earnings, it is clear that this is a very subtle matter and that the burden of a tax policy may be widespread. To suggest the kind of implication we have in mind, we may briefly state and comment upon this famous issue of double taxation.

As ordinarily and simply stated, the issue goes something like this. A corporation pays to the federal government (and usually to the state government as well) an income tax based upon its earnings. Then, when these earnings are disbursed in the form of dividends to stockholders, the stockholders pay an income tax as well. This seems to some especially unfair. Hence the term, double taxation. While most of us think of our incomes as being taxed but once, the stockholders of corporations appear to suffer from an especially severe double taxation.

The argument expressed in this fashion is almost without foundation. While we cannot explore the ramifications of tax policy, we can see some of the holes in the argument by posing another kind of case which we may call quadruple taxation. Thus, the consumers of electric power may be paying higher rates because of a tax on corporate earnings. So, in their electric bills, they are paying some of the cost of federal taxation. They are also, in some states, paying an additional tax based upon the additional sales tax upon their purchases of electricity. This is, of course, double taxation. Moreover, because the consumer's income is taxed, the taxation may be triple. And, if they have earned their income in corporations that are taxed, we may say that their earnings are lower and they are quadrupally taxed. This chain of taxes could be extended to an almost indefinite extent. To state the matter very simply, an employee receives a lower wage because a tax is imposed upon the corporation that pays his wage. He then pays some of that wage out in the form of income tax. He spends some of his wage on goods that are taxed by the state government in the form of a sales tax, and he buys these goods from corporations whose prices are higher because they pay an income tax.

While this illustration is suggested only half seriously, we are completely certain that the question of who bears the burden of any tax must, until carefully analyzed, remain an open one. While research has gone some substantial distance in answering questions about the incidence of taxation, we should be especially wary of believing that merely because a tax appears to impinge on certain incomes it is in fact doing so.

In concluding this section, we may make one more extension of some of the general principles of economic analysis. This extension is the identification of primary causes of given consequences. To illustrate this point, let us assume the following facts: the federal government's budget for a certain year shows a deficit of three billion dollars; a new program of aid to education has cost three billion dollars; an old program of aid to veterans also has cost three billion dollars. Question: Which program caused the deficit?

Our tendency is to say that the new program caused the deficit. Had it not been for the new program, the budget would have been in balance. But what about the old program of three billions of aid to veterans? Had this program not been in effect there would also have been no budget deficit. Or is the deficit a result of a failure of tax revenues to rise sufficiently to cover expenses? Or is it because of the failure of other expenses to fall? The list of "causes" is lengthy and each seems entirely plausible. What can we say?

Fortunately, we can say several things. First, anything as sensitive to many influences as is the federal budget is bound to require several sources of influence to explain its behavior. Second, it is absolutely essential that assumptions be stated as to the behavior of *all* the important sources of influence (variables). It does no good, it is the end of systematic thinking, to treat one or two sources in isolation from the rest of the system. In the illustration of a three billion dollar deficit, for example, we must know several things before we "blame" the new program for the imbalance. At a minimum, we must know that revenues are not less than we had assumed they would be and that other expenses are not higher than we had assumed. Then, and only then, can we meaningfully state the cause of the deficit. And what we finally identify as "the" cause is really the cause only to the extent that our assumptions are valid.

SUMMARY ON LIGHT BULB POLICY

The preceding discussion has presented a general analysis of the economic implications of a particular business policy. Most economists would probably say that the treatment is only the beginning of analysis, that many relationships were omitted, and that those dealt with lacked rigor and specificity. Our aim, however, was to convey perspective, not detailed analysis.

What, then, may the general discussion have achieved?

We have been able to see how the five-fold division of analysis serves the purpose of economic inquiry. Objectives, consumption, output, production, and resources—these identify the locus or position of activities into which we want to look. The fact that these are all related demands that the inquiry be systematic, for their cohesiveness makes the component parts a system. Each part depends upon each other part.

A few of the crucial relationships were mentioned: the relationship of consumption of electricity to price per kilowatt hour, that is, the demand for the output; the relationship of cost to the level of output*; the relationship of profits and taxes to one another and of each to the level of output; the relationship of the quantity of light bulbs supplied to the utility to the cost of such bulbs; and the relationship of other businesses that are potential sellers of bulbs to the levels of output and employment in the utility.

Once we have identified the parts and the important relationships that bind the parts together into a system, once we have recognized the general principle that guides the behavior of the system—then we may analyze the consequences of changes in any of the relationships.

QUESTIONS

CONNECTIONS

1. In one or two sentences, tell what the following things have in common from an economic point of view.
    Iron ore
    Glue
    Cobblestones
    Horses
2. What have the following in common?
    Haircuts
    Appendectomies
    Taxi rides
    Television repairs
3. And the following?
    U.S. trade with Europe
    Vietnam War
    Employment of racial minorities in the U.S.
    U.S. gold stock

---

*You may wonder why the *supply* relationship isn't cited close on the heels of demand. One reason for the omission is that a regulated utility is pretty well bound to meet the quantity of output demanded by consumers at the price set by the regulatory authority, the Public Service Commission. But, as economists know, even in the absence of Commission regulation, a firm holding a monopoly position does not exhibit a supply relationship or schedule in the usual sense of those terms.

ANSWERS

CONNECTIONS

1. All of the four items listed are resources or inputs to a productive activity. Iron ore goes to the steel industry; glue, to the makers of, for example, postage stamps; cobblestones, to the road builders (in earlier times); horses, to agriculture and racing.
   A more peculiar arrangement would make horses the center of attraction. Then, iron ore is the material from which their shoes are made; cobblestones, their highway and glue, their salvage. (I really haven't researched the question of whether glue factories use horses as a raw material.)
2. The four items listed here are all things that consumers buy and are a special category of those things, namely services as contrasted with such goods (tangibles) as automobiles, groceries, and the like.
3. As the reader has discovered, it is very difficult to make connections among these things in a couple of sentences. The following represents my own attempt.

The war in Vietnam has put an enormous strain on our federal budget (to the extent of costing nearly 30 billion dollars a year in 1967) and, as well, involves expenditures overseas, putting a strain on our balance of payments (thereby depleting the gold stock of the country). From these considerations it follows that financing the level of our trade with Europe is increasingly difficult and, also, that the pursuit of domestic policy designed to achieve the employment of racial minorities is threatened because less money is available for domestic spending, and, in addition, the government has less elbow room in pursuing fiscal and monetary policies to achieve full employment.

The special quality of economists' responses showed up in number 3. Here the stress was on the noneconomic factors that bear upon the controversial items listed.

NOTE

The letter below was referred to in this chapter; it provides a few of the facts upon which the analysis of "free" light bulbs was based. The letter came to me in response to my inquiry about whether or not Thomas Edison had bequeathed a sum of money for the purpose of supplying residents of the Detroit area with "free" light bulbs.

I still wonder that my faculty colleague could believe there was such a bequest. But an economist reviewing this book seemed to think I shouldn't wonder. After all, it was merely a question of fact, he said, whether or not Edison left such a legacy. Yet I continue to think it ridiculous—on a par with flying saucers controlled from outer space.

Phlogiston, sweet Afton.

THE DETROIT EDISON COMPANY

OAKLAND DIVISION

BIRMINGHAM OFFICE
220 E MERRILL AVENUE
BIRMINGHAM, MICHIGAN

NOVEMBER 15, 1963

Mr. John E. Maher
Associate Professor of Economics
Oakland University
Rochester, Michigan

Dear Mr. Maher:

I am taking the liberty of answering your letter to Mr. Cisler about a fund of money left by Thomas A. Edison to furnish Michigan residents with free lamp bulbs. This is the first time I have heard this rumor of which there are many involving Mr. Edison.

In 1962 we exchanged 11,556,000 lamp bulbs with an average cost of thirteen cents per lamp. These same lamps would have cost our customers twenty-five cents per lamp on the average if purchased at retail. The cost of these lamps is part of the base on which the residence rate is figured: so there is no basis in fact for this belief.

There are many misconceptions concerning Thomas A. Edison and the electrical industry. The most prevalent is that all companies using the "Edison" name in their title are related corporately so that many customers moving shall we say from Boston Edison Company service area are surprised to find that we have different policies and rates and are in no way connected.

The use of the Edison name in the names of electric utility companies is used to honor the man who made this tremendous industry possible.

                Sincerely,

                P. C. Grant
                Assistant Division Manager

PCG/ef

CHAPTER

7

The Economic System as a Whole

THE preceding chapter about the policy of a single business firm, the Detroit Edison Company, was *microeconomic* in outlook. That is, the discussion was of a relatively small (micro) part of the whole economy. Indeed, most of the earlier writing has been microeconomic. The topics have been about parts of the economy —a business, an industry, a household.

The present chapter, by contrast, lies in the domain of *macroeconomics,* the study of the entire economy. And the entire economy is the sum of all businesses, all households, all governments, and the economic relationships among them. As will be seen, the study of the whole economic system introduces new complexities but it also permits great simplifications. I think that for present, limited purposes, the simplifications far outweigh the new complexities so that the treatment need not be difficult.

Macroeconomics is essentially the study of those larger economic phenomena that are assumed constant for a study of the part of the economy. Macro focuses attention on how large aggregated values are determined: why the national income is of given magnitude, why employment throughout the nation is at certain levels, and why general price and wage levels are what they are. In dynamic studies, it includes the explanation of why these things vary in one way or another—why the economy experiences periods of inflation and deflation, prosperity and depression.

To make the transition from microeconomics to macroeconomics, a few things can be said about the connection between the two areas of inquiry.

Generally, for the study of a part (micro) of the economic system a major assumption is made about the total (macro) economy—namely, that the large economic environment in which the part operates is fixed, given, and unaltered. The particular part under scrutiny is assumed not to affect the large system in any way that is important to analysis. It is assumed, in turn, that no large change takes place in the environment in such a way as to influence the study of the economic part. What are the kinds of economic phenomena that are taken as given when one analyzes a part of the economy? The general level of employment in the economic system together with the level of national income and the average levels of prices and wages are all assumed given and fixed. Constancy in these values is obviously necessary if useful conclusions are to be drawn from analysis of a part of the system. Thus, for example, it would make no sense to say (as we did in the preceding chapter) that consumers will increase their consumption of electricity when the price per kilowatt hour declines if, while saying this, we do not assume that the entire economy is stable. If the entire economy were plunging into the depths of a serious depression, consumption of electricity would *not* increase when the price of electricity fell. This is because, with workers losing their jobs and family incomes dropping, consumers might well curtail their use of electricity despite a reduction in its price.

We conclude that microeconomic analysis assumes that the whole economy is stable (although, of course, this assumption may be relaxed at some of the stages of inquiry).

A second point is this: while the total economy is the sum of its parts, the principles that apply to the parts do not always apply to their sum. On some matters, economic knowledge is fully adequate to explaining why different principles are applicable to the economy as a whole than those that are applicable to its parts. But on other matters, ignorance is the case: economics cannot fully explain the behavior of the whole.

In Chapter 1 we used the contrast between the effects of saving by an individual and the effects of saving by a whole society to show a difference between micro and macroanalysis. Here we may try an illustration from worker productivity.

If an individual worker in a business firm becomes twice as efficient, doing twice as much work in an hour as he used to do, we may expect his employer to reward him handsomely by an increased wage and, perhaps, a promotion. But suppose all the workers in an entire industry become twice as productive; suppose this results in twice the volume of production. May this not cause employers to feel that they need *half* as many workers as before? And may this not lead to widespread unemployment?

This is admittedly an oversimplification. A doubling of worker productivity will probably lower costs of production, yield lower prices for the product, and increase the quantity of output demanded by consumers. But there can be no guarantee—indeed, it is unlikely—that a sufficient increase in production will occur to employ as many workers as before. As labor and management know so well, rising productivity is a threat to employment as well as the source of higher wages and improved living standards. Productivity advances for the individual firm or worker require an analysis different from that applicable to an industry or to the whole economy.

It may be added that it is not only when shifting from the analysis of, say, a single business firm to an analysis of the whole economy that the economist reaches into a different tool box for his principles. *Any* aggregation *may* require a new perspective and new generalizations. Thus, there are some differences in the analyses of industries, geographic regions, and occupations; this is a major reason economists specialize in these kinds of analyses.

In the pages that follow in this chapter, we intend to accomplish two very limited objectives. One is to present a simplified model of the flow of goods and services and money expenditures between households and businesses and the second is to show a simple model of a very few of the relationships that are thought important in governing the economic system. Each of these two

THE ECONOMIC SYSTEM AS A WHOLE

concepts has been developed and refined greatly in recent years, but recent developments and refinements will not be reflected in this abbreviated treatment. Instead, we are interested in portraying what in general is true of those models that attack the problems of the whole economic system. The sole idea is to present important ideas in a form useful for learning and teaching.

THE "LINEAR" FLOW OF INCOME VERSUS THE CIRCULAR FLOW

The earlier representation of economic activity in five parts might be called the "linear" flow of goods and of income. The appropriateness of the word linear is suggested by Figure 7.1. The line at the top with an arrow pointed to the right indicates that some product (like bread) moves from the left where it was in the form of flour, through a production process where labor and other things were added, to become the output, bread. Then it was purchased by a consumer and eaten (consumed) and thereby was transformed into the satisfaction of a human want. Opposite in direction is the flow of money payments indicated by the line at the bottom with an arrow pointed to the left. This line shows that money from consumers who bought the bread flowed leftward to pay for the bread and its production, including the services of resources shown at the extreme left.

Now, as represented here, there is only a one-way connection between what consumers on the right are able to spend on bread and what resource owners on the left receive as income. Thus,

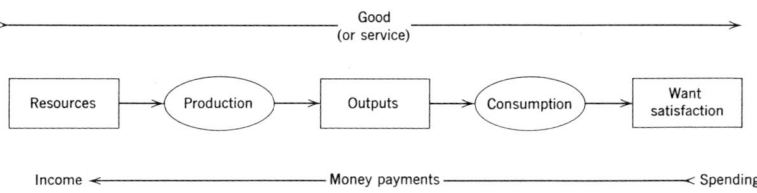

Fig. 7.1

102   WHAT IS ECONOMICS?

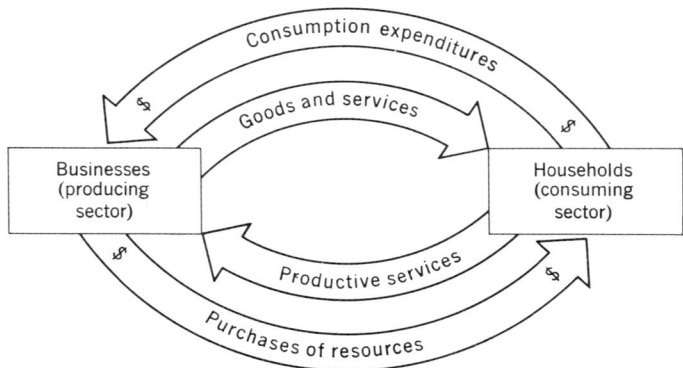

Fig. 7.2   The circular flow of income.

resource owners get their incomes from what consumers spend; but consumers' income doesn't come from what resource owners spend. If we talk about a business, let us say a grocery store, we cannot directly link up the expenditures by people engaged in the productive activity with the revenues of the employing firm. Thus, workers in a grocery store may spend none of their income on purchases made there. Instead, it is highly likely that their expenditures account for no significant fraction of the revenues of the grocery store. The importance of this point comes to the fore when we aggregate for the entire economic system. If we add up *all* economic activities, then we find that there are no "leakages." When we have all economic activities included in our scheme, it becomes true that all of the receipts derived from the sale of goods and services result as income to resource owners; and all of the expenditures by resource owners come out of their incomes earned in the process of production (or are transferred to them from other sectors of the economy).

It is this closure which leads to the use of the term "closed system" in referring to the aggregate of all economic activity in the national economy. As depicted in Figure 7.2 below, we see that there are principally two sectors of the economy (neglecting government) and that the expenditures by households on the right in the upper loop of the diagram provide all of the income that business receives; and that all of the expenditures by business on resources come from these receipts as represented in the flow at the bottom of the diagram. This is the circular flow of expenditures in the economy. Counter to this circular flow of payments is the flow of goods and services purchased by households from business (upper loop, clockwise) and, at the bottom of the diagram, the flow of productive resources (the services of land, labor, and capital) from households to business (lower loop).

There is a close similarity between this circular flow and the "linear," five-part scheme advanced earlier. The linear depiction began with resources, here more accurately termed "Productive services;" next came production, here shown as "Businesses (producing sector);" then, in the earlier figure, output, here, "Goods and services." Consumption and want satisfaction were the last two stages in the initial classification and these, together, are subsumed within "Households (consuming sector)." In the labeling, the circular flow diagram is virtually identical to the former scheme, differing only in emphasizing institutional and social arrangements. In conception, the striking difference is the matter of the closed, circular system versus the open, linear one.

The circular flow of income is analogous to a great vending machine, as mentioned earlier in this book. Imagine that in this vending machine there are a capitalist representing the millions of owners of businesses in this country and a laborer representing the millions of workers. These two together during a time we shall call a productive day are at work within the vending machine, creating the goods and services that they hope consumers will want. But we state at the outset for the purpose of this little analogy that these two heroes of our drama are, in fact, the consumers themselves.

When the productive day is ended, our two actors divide the money that is in the till from the preceding day's activities, leave the vending machine by the back door, and go home to wash, change, and assume their roles as consumers. In the time period we shall call the consuming evening, our two actors return to the front of the vending machine as consumers demanding the goods and services that earlier they produced. They put into the various slots of the vending machine their nickels, dimes, and quarters to indicate their preferences for the various kinds of goods and services they see displayed and, having enjoyed a consuming orgy, return home to sleep and prepare for work on the following day.

This little analogy contains a major insight into economic analysis. First of all, we see that it is generally true that the same people who produce the goods and services are those who consume them. Each of us generally has a role as producer and consumer. Second, we see that costs of production, namely, what was paid out of the till at the end of the "productive day," is the income of the resource owners, labor and capital. It is from this very income that the producers and consumers during the "consuming evening" make their expenditures to buy that which they have produced. It is obvious that if we repeated this process of a productive day and a consuming night there would be a circular flow of money and of goods and services. The two flows, of course, are opposite in direction; that is, the money goes to the factors of production in the form of income and, from the back of the machine, enters the front as the demand for goods and services. The goods and services, on the other hand, flow in the opposite direction; that is, the factors of production render services when they enter the back of the machine at the beginning of the productive day, and the goods and services produced leave the front of the machine upon being demanded by the consumers.

Without our developing the model any further, we can see that it is an important vehicle for advancing our understanding of economic affairs. Just by suggesting a series of questions we can show how it is possible to shed light on major economic events. Suppose, for example, the amount spent by the consumers as they appear in front of our vending machine is less than sufficient to buy what was produced during the productive day. What will happen? Obviously, inventories will pile up and the management of our productive machine may find it necessary to reduce employment, to cut the hours of labor or to lay off workers in order to bring a better balance between the volume of production and the level of expenditures. Another line of inquiry is the following: Suppose that the amount of expenditures by consumers on what was produced during the preceding day is augmented by "new purchasing power." That is, suppose that while at given prices the volume of expenditures has been just sufficient to re-

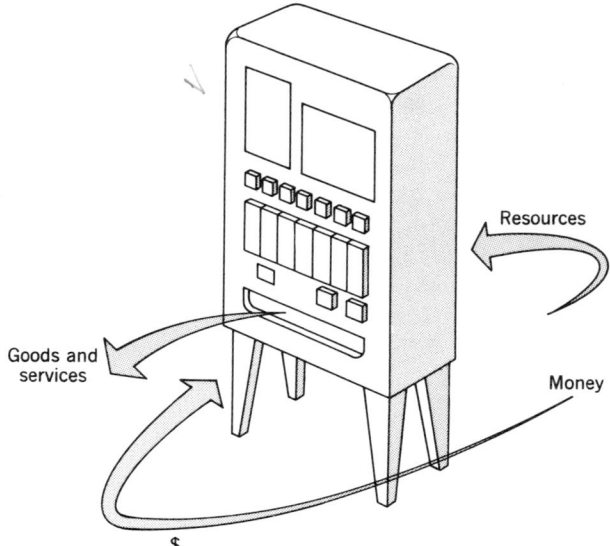

Fig. 7.3 Vending machine: analogy to flow of money, goods, and services in the whole economy.

move from the vending machine all that was produced during the preceding day, a consumer appears with extra money that perhaps he got from a bank loan. What will happen now? There is a larger volume of expenditures than previously, and upward pressure will be exerted upon prices.

This little illustration of the circular flow, depicted in Figure 7.3, is a highly useful device for studying business fluctuations and the influence of government upon the economy. While we have not explicitly introduced the role of government, its effects can be included within this simple model.

A NATIONAL INCOME MODEL

The idea of national income and its circular flow is one of the cleverest ever devised by economists. Despite difficulties in definition and measurement, the use of this key idea has made it possible to tell whether an economy is performing near capacity, whether expansion or contraction faces the nation, and how growth in one nation compares with growth in another.

Use of national income estimates was greatly accelerated after the publication of John Maynard Keynes' revolutionary book, *The General Theory of Employment Interest and Money*.* Almost all discussions of how an economy's national income gets to be what it is from one time to another derive from Keynes' work. The simple, brief excursion in the paragraphs below is a simplification of these same, basic ideas.

To present a simple model of how an economy's income gets determined, all that is needed are three things: a definition, a relationship, and a fact. The definition is that the income of an economy consists of the value of the goods and services that consumers buy (Consumption) and the goods that businesses buy—factories, equipment, machinery (Investment). Neglecting the purchases of governments and of foreigners, income for, say, a year, is the sum of expenditures by consumers and businesses during the year. Earlier discussion of the circular flow of income makes clear why these expenditures which result in wages, profits, and rents are equal to national income. This definition of income is the first of the three things we need for a model of the economy. (We neglect differences between net and gross income.)

Excluded from this definition are expenditures on old items that were not produced during the period for which we are accounting. Thus, a 1929 Model A Ford that was manufactured and sold in 1929 was counted in that year's national income. Even if it is sold again this year, it does not count in this year's income for that would be counting the same value more than once. Similarly, sales of things like land, which are not "produced," do not count in the expenditures by consumers and businesses that are reckoned a part of national income. Only things produced in the current year are counted in the income of the current year. Again, the circular flow and the vending machine analogy serve to sort out those values that count and those that do not count in national income.

---

* New York: Harcourt Brace, 1936.

Besides the definition of income, one relationship is necessary in order to get a model that will give the value of national income. This relationship is the "consumption function," named by Keynes. The relationship states that consumption expenditures depend upon the level of national income. To keep the illustration as simple as is possible, it will be assumed here that the level of consumption expenditures is always eight-tenths of the level of income, that is, consumers always spend an amount equal to eight-tenths of national income. The other two-tenths of their income they save.

A definition and a relationship have now been given. The last thing necessary is a piece of information, namely, the level of investment spending by business. We may assume as a fact, for example, that investment spending is known to be 20 billion dollars. Now how can the three things—definition, relationship, and fact—be put together to tell what the national income is?

First, the definition: national income is the sum of consumer spending and business spending. The relationship informs us that eight-tenths of income is consumption; therefore (by subtraction), two-tenths must be business spending. If two-tenths of income is business spending (investment) and business spending is known to be 20 billion dollars, then national income must be five times as much or 100 billion dollars (5 times 20 billion dollars).

The same deduction can be made through algebra in the following fashion.

Definition:	Income (Y) is the sum of Consumption (C) and Investment (I)	$Y = C + I$
Relationship: (Consumption Function)	Consumption is eight-tenths as much as Income	$C = .8Y$
Known fact:	Investment is 20 billion dollars	$I = 20$

Then, substituting $C = .8Y$ in the equation $Y = C + I$ gives:

$$Y = .8Y + I$$

therefore

$$Y - .8Y = I$$
$$.2Y = I$$

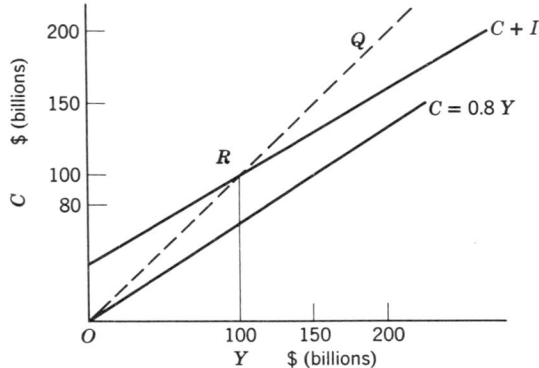

Fig. 7.4 Graphic determination of the level of national income (Y).

and if $I = 20$, then

$$.2Y = 20$$
$$Y = 100$$

That is, national income is 100 billion dollars.

A final way of showing the same determination of the level of national income is represented in Figure 7.4. There we see a two-dimensional chart: Consumption (C) is measured along the vertical axis in billions of dollars and Income (Y) is measured along the horizontal axis. The dashed line labeled Q is only a reference line showing the location of equal values for Y and C. The consumption function is labeled $C = .8Y$ and locates all the places where Consumption is eight-tenths as much as income. Now, to find where income (Y) will be if Investment (I) is 20 billion dollars, we have only to add to all the Consumption values the amount, 20 billion. This gives the line labeled $C + I$ which is parallel to $C = .8Y$ at a height of 20 above it. Where this $C + I$ line intersects the reference line at point R on line Q is the level of national income; the level is read along the horizontal axis as 100 billion dollars. Only at the intersection at point R does the sum of Consumption and Investment equal national Income.*

---

* The reader who has perused the treatment of this topic in a modern textbook will probably be struck by my omission of saving from the discussion. And, indeed, most treatments would have added two notions to my

Three demonstrations have been given of the same simple model of the economy, a model for determining the level of national income: a verbal, a mathematical, and a geometrical demonstration. All three show the same result, that from a definition, a relationship, and a (assumed) fact, the resulting national income is a specific magnitude—in this case, 100 billion dollars.

Now, of course, things in the "real" world are more complicated than this simple model might lead us to believe. The consumption function is an estimate of behavior and it relates consumption to consumers' disposable (after-tax) income, not directly to national income. Tax relations have to be considered in a full-blown model; so, too, does the level of government expenditures require inclusion. Moreover, interest rates and price movements need to be considered along with the supplies of resources, especially the supply of labor. Yet, the omission of all these important matters does not vitiate the central propositions of definition and relationship which are the basis for the modern theory of the determination of the level of national income.*

Along with the analysis of national income, the study of money and banking comprises a vast portion of the area of macroeconomics. Any text in economics would devote several chapters both to income and to money and banking. But, as repeated in these pages, this book is not a text. It is, rather, a guide to economics. Therefore, we are compelled to let this brief discussion represent, however inadequately, most of the field of macroeconomics.

---

exposition: first, that income minus consumption equals saving (i.e., $Y - C = S$); second, savings equals investment by definition ($S = I$). As important as these twin notions are to a more extended treatment, I hope the reader will congratulate me for my succinctness instead of upbraiding me for my unorthodoxy. The fact is that these additional notions are not necessary. In mathematical language, they "overdetermine" the system.

* I think I have successfully resisted the temptation to "cover" all of the macroeconomic inferences that can be derived from the model just discussed. Yet I shall weaken in this footnote to the extent of admitting that the famous multiplier—which has kept classroom instructors busy for hours each semester—is easily comprehended in the model. The multiplier is defined as the reciprocal of the "marginal propensity to save." Here the saving propensity is two-tenths; its reciprocal is 5, the value of the multiplier. As the reader can show, a multiplier of 5 means that for every dollar increase in investment (I), national income (Y) will rise by five dollars.

WHAT? HOW? FOR WHOM?

The brief glimpse we have taken of macroeconomics provides a convenient opportunity to consider three of the major functions attributed to the economic system. While there is slight danger that in some contexts this formulation of function may be burdened with some anthropomorphic interpretation, it is nevertheless helpful to our organization of thought about the economic system to consider these functions.

Generally, it is recognized that partial answers to three major questions are provided by an economy. These questions are: What shall be produced? How shall it be produced? For whom shall it be produced?

Of course, before entering the economic domain, we should notice at the outset that no *single* discipline serves fully to show how answers to these questions are determined. For example, the whole matter of culture in determining the tastes of the population bears heavily upon the question, What shall be produced? Similarly, habit, law, and tradition affect both the what and the how as well as the for whom. Americans typically want Christmas trees or Chanukah candles in December, largely for religious reasons that are transmitted from generation to generation by customary observance of the holidays. So, in the following treatment, where we single out the economic analysis that contributes to answering this trilogy of questions, we should not forget the partial nature of the answers.

Returning to our circular flow or vending machine analogy, we notice that it is the expenditures of consumers that largely determine what shall be produced. This is the meaning of consumer sovereignty, an essential feature of a market-directed society. As the consumer purchases the various goods and services produced by the economy, he is casting what we may call "dollar votes" in favor of the production of certain things and, by abstaining from expenditures on certain items, he is voting negatively against their production. Consumers, then, in making expenditures in the marketplaces help to direct the production of business firms into those lines of activity which they, the consumers, favor.

The how of production—how shall things be produced?—is answered principally by the business firms that are the producers. To achieve economy in production, the firms' managers combine the resources discussed earlier in those ways provided by technology that maximize the profits of the producing firm and (under competitive circumstances) minimize the costs of production. This is the major reason for the much heralded efficiency that is thought to typify an economic system characterized by competitive firms.

The "for whom shall goods be produced" question is answered in the market place for the resources of production. As business firms bid for the services of land, labor, and capital, they are in fact offering incomes for the services rendered by these factors. Since the producers are seeking to produce at lowest cost, they will tend to hire the most productive factors, and those factors will have incomes proportionate to their productivity. The more productive for the employing firm the factor is in a market sense, the higher will tend to be its income.*

---

* Cf. Calderwood, *Op. cit.*, wherein a fuller discussion of this important matter is taken up.

There should be noted several qualifications to the proposition that consumers' wishes are followed in a private enterprise market economy and also to the deduction that this economy most efficiently allocates resources. One of these qualifications arises, of course, because many industries are not characterized by a high degree of competition. That is, a few producers dominate the field and there is a deviation from the ideal posited by the competitive system. Second, the "true" social costs of production may be inadequately mirrored in the accounting ledgers of the firm. A single example will serve to illustrate this point. A chemical manufacturer located on a river may keep very good books reflecting its costs but it is unable to show what costs may arise from its pollution of the river. Elsewhere in the economy, costs are borne by fishermen who seek in vain to enjoy their sport, by bathers, and by others. But the sacrifice made by these persons, or indeed the money outlays expended by a municipality in the attempt to clean up the river, may not be directly associated with the chemical production going on in the firm. A third matter concerning the ideal allocation of resources arises simply because of the question about whether consumers are rational in their choices and whether even if they are rational they are able to act independently of the producers whose advertising bombards them. It is obviously a dangerous

Now, of course, governments, trade unions, and other organizations serve importantly to modify the allocation of resources that would take place in a more highly competitive system. For example, minimum wage laws enacted by Congress and state legislatures and the collective bargaining practices of trade unions limit, in important respects, the determinations that would be made in the marketplace. Moreover, social welfare programs, in a large sense, together with social insurance schemes further modify the market. Thus, for example, the American people have agreed that a worker upon reaching age 65 should not have his income determined exclusively by market forces but, under Social Security legislation, should be guaranteed a minimum retirement income. In these and other ways the decisions emanating from the market place are modified. For this reason the American economy is most accurately characterized as a "mixed" economy, one in which determinations in marketplaces are mixed with an active role for government and for other organizations.

QUESTIONS

QUID PRO QUO

1. "If the federal government borrows a lot of money from the public, this borrowing is almost certain to be inflationary."
   The preceding statement is
   (a) true
   (b) false
   (c) impossible to judge
2. "If the federal government loans a lot of money to the public, this lending is almost certain to be inflationary."
   The preceding statement is
   (a) true
   (b) false
   (c) impossible to judge

---

tautology to say that consumers' wishes are followed in the allocation of resources if these wishes are largely determined by the hucksters on television and in the other mass media. While other qualifications to the optimum allocation of resources may be advanced, these are a few of the more salient ones.

ANSWERS

QUID PRO QUO

1. It is not *borrowing* but *spending* that chiefly affects price levels. Hence, the answer is: (b) false.

The root cause of inflation lies in increases in spending that exceed increases in production. Sometimes this is colorfully expressed as "too much money chasing too few goods." While there may be other causes of inflation, this would seem to be the primary one. From this assumption, it follows that borrowing in itself is not a cause for inflation and may even result in the opposite effect, namely, deflation. For example, if the federal government borrows a lot of money from the public, the public has *less* money to spend and therefore its spending may fall and exert downward pressure on prices. Now, of course, the government has more money to spend, and therefore the crucial question for inflation is whether the government spends the money at a more rapid rate than the public would have spent it (not whether it has come into possession of the money). This may seem like a fine point, but its importance has been demonstrated rather conclusively by Lerner and others, and it is essential to an understanding of monetary and fiscal policy. See A. P. Lerner, *The Economics of Control* (New York: Macmillan, 1944).

2. Essentially the same answer applies to "2" as to "1": (b) false.

Again, it is not *lending* but *spending* that generates inflation, although it must immediately be conceded that most people borrow in order to spend, and therefore borrowing and lending, as discussed above, may lead to inflation. Still, both of these statements, as they stand, are false because they say these processes are *"almost certain* to be inflationary."

The replies of my fellow economists clearly repudiate my analysis! I can only report the distribution of choices (in percentages).

1. (a) 3
   (b) 22
   (c) 75
2. (a) 16
   (b) 10
   (c) 74

CHAPTER

8

Organization of Economic Knowledge

THIS book presents one view of what economics is and of how economic knowledge may be organized. We have looked at other views that are fraught with misconception and have applied economic analysis to a small problem, hoping to show in practice what had been set down as theory. A few generalizations were offered about the whole economy, the sum of all economic activities.

It is now appropriate to spend some time on two important, complementary themes: first, some valid, alternative ways of ordering economic knowledge; and second, the unifying roles of accounting and statistics in the study of economics.

Any body of thought can be organized in a number of useful ways. One way might be called, "Who said what and when?" This is a kind of intellectual history and has proved attractive to philosophers, political scientists, and theologians, as well as to economists whose specialty is the history of economic doctrine.

Another way of sorting a group of ideas is by major areas of application. The natural sciences lend themselves to this and we find books, journals, and courses at universities devoted to electrical engineering, chemical engineering, and mechanical engineering; chemistry, electricity, and mechanics are applied in the service of special inquiry. For economics, this is like the areas of social policy: money and banking, industrial organization, and labor economics.

In this chapter, however, the point is to begin by looking at a mathematical organization of economics, noticing a couple of hybrid organizations, and then at a classification bearing institutional (societal) significance. The reason for doing this is to show other ways of dissecting the science, ways that may well supplement (or perhaps, for some readers, displace) the method advocated in these pages. In any case, the strengths and weaknesses of one approach are better understood in comparison with other approaches.

MATHEMATICAL, CLASSICAL AND INSTITUTIONAL SCHOOLS

Professor Samuelson, one of the most influential economists of our time, has worked out a highly systematic order for economics in his book, *Foundations of Economic Analysis*.* The basis upon which Samuelson creates his economic order is heralded on the title page of the book where the motto appears, "Mathematics is a Language." The chapters of the work, often highly mathematical, combine two criteria for delineating the subject matter. On the one hand, some chapters deal with those areas of economic inquiry that are best understood through their common *mathematical properties*. On the other hand, some chapters are organized according to the more usual *applications* of economic analysis; there is, for example, a chapter on production, one on consumer behavior, and another on welfare economics. These two criteria, common mathematical properties and applications, prove to be efficient guides for Samuelson's advancement of economic knowledge.

---

* Cambridge: Harvard University Press, 1947.

It is worth while to look more closely at the first of these two ways of organizing the science.

Certain mathematical properties are common to a wide range of problems in economics. As illustration, we may cite problems of maximizing (or minimizing). A business firm may be considered a profit-maximizing activity that is governed by the principle that things are going well when the difference between revenues and costs is greatest. This difference is, in fact, the definition of profits. In a formal sense, the behavior of a satisfaction-maximizing consumer is closely analogous to that of the business firm. Now, if we can sort out the relationships that are common to both business and consumer, we can examine these all in one fell swoop. It is here that the power of mathematics is greatest; it makes no difference to a general economic theory of the maximizing process what the *content* of an economic problem or proposition is, provided that rigorous algebraic statements can be made about the significant relationships. The "X" and "Y" can be the money revenues and costs of a business or the apples and oranges of a satisfaction-maximizing consumer. What is important is the mathematics of maximizing.

We have earlier dealt with the important idea of equilibrium, defined roughly as a situation in which the further reallocation of resources does not improve the attainment of a stated objective. In our example of the student seeking a high grade average in two subjects, equilibrium meant that no further shift of hours of study from one subject to another would improve his average grade. This idea of equilibrium is another idea that finds convenient mathematical expression and Samuelson, in the work referred to, makes extensive use of such expression to organize his inquiry into the implications of equilibrium. Again, it does not matter whether we consider the equilibrium of a consumer, business, or economy; there are enough formal properties in common to permit useful deductions to be made.

The great potential for a mathematical organization of economics should not be underrated. All of the propositions of economics can be organized under those branches of mathematics that are the most powerful in permitting deduction. Yet there are dangers that arise from this procedure, some of them alluded to earlier. Unlike some of the more doctrinaire among both his followers and critics, Samuelson recognizes that economics is not the same thing as mathematics. Both the motto, referred to before, and such transitional passages as the following make this clear: ". . . but the corresponding theorem is definitely untrue. Economically this is not hard to visualize." And there follows an economic, in this case a verbalized, statement of an earlier mathematical deduction.*

It seems unnecessary to point out why the present writing is not mathematically presented or why the kinds of problems dealt with here are different from those found in a contribution to economic theory.

Far earlier in the development of economic science and reaching into the present century, influencing today's textbooks, is the orthodox division of economic knowledge into four areas: production, consumption, distribution, and exchange. It is obvious that the present writing has adopted the first two of these categories and has lumped together the last two under what we have been calling "relationships." In our schematic representations, the use of the two categories of resources and outputs is only an extension of production.

What differences there are between the classical organization of economics and our "fivefold" division arise chiefly from our emphasis on pedagogical convenience, a wider definition of the science, and the view that attention should be called to the mortar uniting the chief processes of economic activity, that is, the set of relationships. This focus upon relationships, arbitrary in some ways, has more in common with a mathematical approach to study than with the classical organization.**

---

* *Ibid,* p. 354. See also Chapter VIII, "Welfare Economics." Compare with the following from his principles text: ". . . knowledge of mathematics itself is needed only for the higher reaches of economic theory. Logical reasoning is the key to success in the mastery of economic principles, and shrewd weighing of empirical evidence is the key to success in the mastery of economic applications." *Economics* (New York: McGraw-Hill, 5th edition, 1961), p. 8.

** Another succinct statement of the organization of economics is contained in Professor Robbins' famous essay cited above, p. 25. The brilliant generality of Robbins' scheme, his correction of the mistakes of earlier theorists, and his consistency with the main lines of classical thought are all worthy of note. Since his effort antedates both the rise of the macroeconomics we

Different from the systematic attempts thus far commented on is the division of economics according to emphasis upon economic theory and allied disciplines. Implicitly, the present writing has already suggested the nature of this approach. It consists essentially in recognizing something called economics, something else called institutionalism (or institutional economics), and something called mathematical economics. As economists know so well, these terms used to be battle cries for many professors of one or another of the three faiths.

We cannot pretend to have dealt adequately with this threefold division. Since institutionalism has been the most slighted, however, a few words about it are in order.

Conditions of scarcity determine economic value. Whatever is difficult to obtain (supply) and much wanted (demand) is scarce and has value. The greater the difficulty and the more it is wanted, the greater the value. Economics is largely occupied with variations on this theme. But it is not only production and consumption processes and their interrelationships that set the conditions of scarcity and, therefore, determine value. Custom, law, and ideology play important roles as well. Land has value because of legal protections to private property; city zoning ordinances have created and destroyed land values. Trade union practices and collective bargaining contracts have reshuffled wages. Government tax policies have made and unmade businesses. All this is known and accepted. But is the study of this kind of institutional influence properly the same as economics?

A reasonable answer would seem to be, no: the study of institutions is an essential adjunct to economics—as economics is an essential adjunct to the study of institutions. Each is the *ceteris paribus* (other things being equal) of the other, but only the student who knows something about the *ceteris* (other things) can safely operate on the assumption of *paribus* (being equal). The rise of the labor movement has important implications for such values as wages and "orthodox" economic explanation that

---

associate with Keynes and the fuller development of mathematical economics, his writing omits a treatment of these developments. More positively stated, his essay is largely microeconomic in spirit; and he seems now to have been unduly pessimistic about the fruitfulness of investigations of the economy as a whole.

neglected this institution would be sorely deficient. Equally deficient would be an institutional explanation that neglected the scarcity relationships. Economics and institutionalism, reasonably construed, are different but wholly complementary. Bad writing, dogmatism, ignorance, and jealousy are largely responsible for the wars that earlier raged between exponents of these different views. But as the dust has settled, the work of John R. Commons, institutionalist of the Wisconsin School, still looks pretty good. So, too, do the works of the economists cited earlier.

ECONOMIC ACCOUNTING

We now turn to one of the neatest unifying themes that runs throughout much of the study and practice of economic science. This theme is economic accounting.* A science itself, economic accounting provides the framework within which economic values and the sectors of their origin may be rigorously analyzed.

Consider the idea of cost and its particular manifestation as wages. To the *economist*, a sum of wages is the measure of the relative scarcity of a primary resource, namely, labor. The economist, doubling as *statistician*, will deal with this sum as a mathematically determined sample whose significance depends on such matters as the frequency distribution of the population from which it was selected. Whether the sum is accurate enough to be relied upon is a question for the statistician to decide. The *economic accountant* will specify where this sum becomes an entry in the accounts that will measure economic performance.

Without the accounting framework there is no possibility of discovering if an actual economic process is efficient or inefficient; whether profits or losses are being incurred; whether the balance of payments is in deficit or surplus; whether national income is rising or falling; whether on balance the monetary system is piling up claims or destroying them; whether the expansion of

---

* Another theme is statistics. The relations of accounting to statistics and of both to economics are worth detailed exploration by students of methodology. Unfortunately, I am unequally short of time, space, and competence for such an undertaking.

one industry is adding to, or detracting from the expansion of other industries.*

We shall give a little example of the uses of several of these ways of accounting, choosing to omit only the balance of payments. Let us take the following few assumed facts.

A boy who shines shoes has 20 customers in the course of four hours. He charges $.25 for each shoeshine and half his customers pay him cash, half use their credit, i.e., they owe him the money. During the four hours, he uses up half a can of polish and buys another can for $.60. Also, after servicing his customers, he builds a box to hold his cleaning and shining equipment, a box arbitrarily valued at $3. There are no taxes or other expenses.

Using the first of our accounting systems, we determine the profit (or loss) for this business. Receipts from the enterprise are $5 (20 sales at $.25 apiece—even though not all the customers paid cash). Expenses were $.30 (half a can of polish at $.60 a can). Subtracting expenses from receipts gives us net income of $4.70. The income account might look like this.

Receipts	$5.00
Less expenses for materials	.30
Net income	$4.70

The amount of $4.70 might be what our entrepreneur would call "profit." But let us be somewhat more accurate. We assume the young businessman knows that his labor is worth about $1.00 an hour; if he worked as a delivery boy, that is what he would earn. In this case, the 4 hours he devoted to shining shoes are valued at $4.00. (Note this value is an opportunity cost.) Therefore, this amount of wages should properly be subtracted from the net income of the business to arrive at profits. So we rewrite the income account for the business firm to show this:

---

* It may be remarked that I have tried here to represent the five kinds of accounts in widest use; business accounts, balance of payments, national income accounts, flow-of-funds accounts, and input-output accounts. Other accounting systems, together with the stock versus flow distinction, are highly important but need not detain us here.

Receipts	$5.00
Less expenses for materials	.30
	$4.70
Less Wages	4.00
Profit	$ .70

The profit figure is probably the most significant if we wish to judge the economic efficiency of this enterprise. To guage efficiency, we might compare this profit with that earned in other businesses making due allowance for amounts of capital equipment invested and the risks involved.

Now, we may turn from business accounting to a national income accounting framework and ask, "What was the contribution of this firm to society's national income?" To answer this, we need to add up the value of all the services that were rendered. One service was labor: 4 hours valued at $4. Another service was rendered by capital: $.70 of profit. Our "national income account" looks like this:

Wages	$4.00
Profits	.70
Income originating in firm	$4.70

However, there is an additional value to be included, namely, the value of the box the entrepreneur built to hold his equipment. You will recall that this was arbitrarily valued at $3. A full statement of the contribution of the business to national income is $7.70.

Wages	$4.00
Profits	.70
Added to capital	3.00
Total income originating in firm	$7.70

(We note parenthetically that if there had been a using up of equipment during the 4 hours, that is, depreciation of capital,

WHAT IS ECONOMICS?

this would have to be subtracted from "Added to capital." Moreover, since depreciation is an item of expenses, the profit statement for the firm would have to be rewritten. Expenses would be increased by the amount of depreciation and profits, therefore, would be reduced by that amount.)

QUESTION

WHERE DID IT GO?

The concept of the gross national product (GNP) from the preceding chapter may be applied to the numerical example of the operation of the shoeshine business, just discussed. All we have to do is treat the business as though it were a whole economy.

In the example, the GNP appears to be $8. Its composition is:

Consumer expenditures	$5.00
(on shoeshines)	
Business expenditures	3.00
(on capital, i.e.,	
the shoeshine box)	
Apparent GNP	$8.00

Question. How do we account for the $.30 difference between the apparent GNP of $8 and the national income of $7.70?

ANSWER

WHERE DID IT GO?

The difference of $.30 is the decrease in inventory of shoe polish used up in the process of production. The true GNP is $7.70, the same as national income. (If there had been depreciation, as earlier mentioned, then there would have been a difference between GNP and national income equal to the amount of depreciation.)

The "sales" side of the GNP for the shoeshine firm looks like this:

$5.00	Consumption
3.00	Investment
− .30	Inventory decrease
$7.70	GNP

An even more detailed accounting would treat the purchase of $.60 of polish as a purchase from "abroad" and arrive at the same GNP as follows:

$5.00	Consumption
3.00	Investment
.60	Inventory additions
− .30	Inventory decreases
− .60	Purchases from "abroad"
$7.70	GNP

In our example in the text, we left out the inventory addition of $.60 arising from the purchase of polish because it was conveniently offset by $.60 of purchases from "abroad" and therefore had no net effect on GNP or income.

This question was not prepared in time for submission to the economists who were polled for most of the other questions.

We turn now to an accounting for the flow of cash in the enterprise. Receipts from sales amounted to $5. But only half this sum was cash. The other half was like I.O.U.'s, that is, promises to pay or accounts receivable. However, because the firm bought $.60 worth of polish, cash on hand is different from cash receipts. Let us say the business opened with cash on hand of $8. Cash received was $2.50, so cash on hand rose to $10.50. Then, when the polish was purchased, it fell to $9.90. If we imagine that our businessman keeps the firm's money in one pocket and his own wages in another, we may deduct $4 of wages from the pocket where cash on hand for the business is kept, leaving $5.90 in the business and $4 in the wage pocket.

We should at this point stop moving numbers around and notice the purpose of keeping track of the flow of cash. For a business or an individual, cash represents a unique form of purchasing power. Some things must be bought for cash. The "accounts receivable" cannot easily be spent to buy groceries or pay the piper. And this is true for the whole economy. Promises to pay must generally be turned into money before they can be used to make purchases. If the government or business wishes to know whether the economy has enough purchasing power to sustain an economic expansion, it must look at the cash position of major sectors of the economy—households, businesses, and governments.

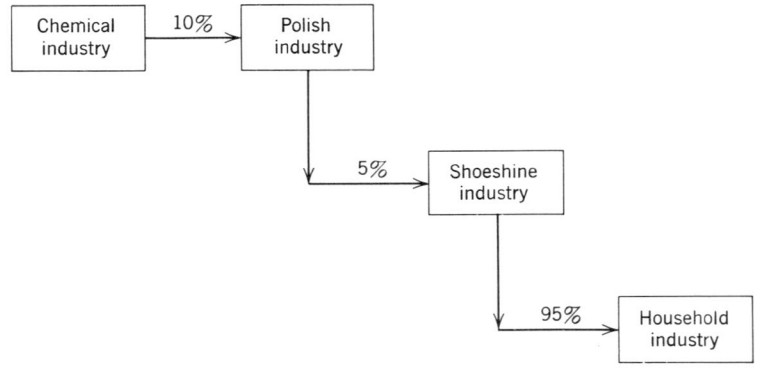

Fig. 8.1

We may add that, for an economy, "cash" means deposits in checking accounts primarily and, secondarily, folding money and coins.

We have now illustrated in simple fashion the use of three kinds of accounting for a business activity: profit (or loss), national income originating in the business, and cash flows. Figure 8.1 may serve to show the so-called "input-output" accounting which is sometimes referred to as "interindustry economics." In our example, we shall not need the numerical values used earlier.

Let us imagine four "industries" in a sequence; all of them related to the shoeshining industry. First is the chemical industry. This one supplies materials used by the second, namely, the shoe polish industry. Third is the shoeshining industry itself. This is the one from which all the preceding accounting examples were chosen. Last is the household industry (or sector) upon whose shoes the polish is ultimately put. The sequence of materials flow is depicted below from the chemical industry on the left to the household industry on the right.

The percentages in the figure require explanation. The first percentage means that 10 percent of the chemical industry's production goes into the shoe polish industry. The next figure means that 5 percent of the production of the polish industry goes into the shoeshine industry. The last figure says that 95 percent of

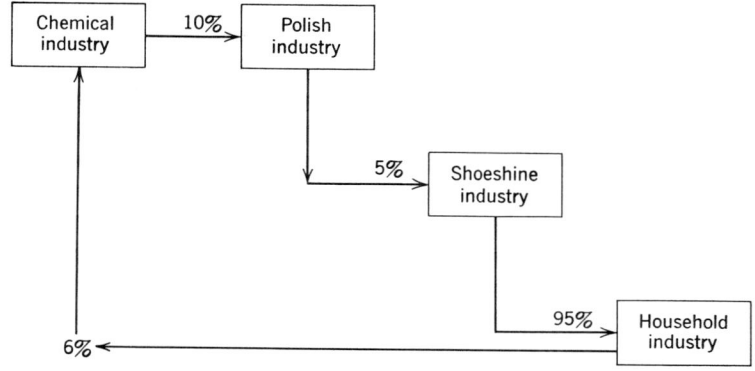

Fig. 8.2

the production of the shoeshining industry is bought by households (or consumers).

Finally, to make a complete circuit, we add to the diagram an arrow showing that 6 percent of the "production" of households goes into the chemical industry. This addition is shown in Figure 8.2. The new relationship simply means that 6 percent of the workers in the economy are employed in the chemical industry, since the "production" of a household is, in this case, chiefly the rendering of services to industry.*

The last step we shall undertake here in representing input-output analysis is to show a more complete "closed" system. This requires recognition of the fact that households supply labor to

---

* In our simplified presentation, we are skipping over the difficult problems of defining units and their measurement. We are not here representing a single, circular flow by which labor services are turned into chemicals which are then transformed into shoe polish, which then gets made into shined shoes. It is probably better to think of discrete jumps at each step in the kind of thing called "production."

In the actual tables used by economists, the economy is divided into scores of industries. Moreover, the kinds of connections shown among industries include not only the percentage distribution of output, but the price connection, the effects of changes in efficiency (productivity), and the derivation of investment (and savings). The government and relevant foreign production are included as major sectors.

all industries, that there are many other industries than those we have represented, and that most of the other industries supply one another with some of their production. To close the system, we simply add a new classification called "Other Industries" to our list of four and depict all the flows of production that may take place.

Table 8.1, organized like a multiplication table, lists at the top and side our five industries. If we read across the first row, we get the percentage distribution of the Chemical Industry's pro-

Table 8.1 Percentage Distribution of the Selected Output of Five Industries

	Chemical Industry	Polish Industry	Other Industries	Shoeshine Industry	Household Industry
Chemical industry	4	10	50	6	30
Polish industry				5	
Other industries				1	
Shoeshine industry				2	
Household industry	6			1	

duction among the five industries: chemicals takes 4 percent of its own output, sends on 10 percent to the Polish Industry, 50 percent to Other Industries, 6 percent to the Shoeshine Industry and 30 percent to Households. (All figures are, of course, hypothetical.) Each row is read in identical fashion. The column headed Shoeshine Industry, for example, is read as follows, from top to bottom: the industry takes 6 percent of the Chemical Industry's output, 5 percent of the Polish Industry's output, 1 percent of the output of Other Industries, 2 percent of its own output, and 1 percent of the output of Households. (The only other numbers we have put into the table are those mentioned in the previous discussion.)

We have spent more time on developing the idea of an input-output table for two reasons: it is generally less familiar than the sets of accounts already mentioned, and it represents one of the most powerful new instruments of economic analysis.* In Chapter 3, "Some Achievements of Economics," we touched upon a military application of input-output. Here we may cite a second kind of application, underscoring the pedagogical power of this scheme.

Referring to our simplified table, suppose we want to know what the consequences to other industries will be if we expand production in the Shoeshine Industry by 10 percent. Since shoeshining takes 6 percent of the output of chemicals, we know that the chemical industry must expand output by around six-tenths of a percent (6 percent of 10 percent). We are alerted immediately to the need for knowing whether resources are available to the Chemical Industry. Is the industry already operating at full capacity? Are there shortages in the supply of certain kinds of workers? Will resources have to be shifted to chemicals from other industries? The same kind of calculations may be made for each of the other industries that supplies the Shoeshine Industry. An adequate appreciation of the total effect of expansion (or contraction) in any industry can only be arrived at by this kind of analysis of structural relationships among industries.

CONCLUSION

It might be thought that this matter of accounting can safely be left to the accountants and to those economists who feel a need to categorize values empirically derived. Then the student of economics is left free to concentrate on scarcity relationships more abstractly conceived. But this is dangerous to an understanding of economics.

It is dangerous because many economic relationships are diffi-

---

* While the concept of input-output goes back to the Physiocrats in France in the last quarter of the eighteenth century, the idea lay fallow for about 150 years. Then, in the early nineteen-thirties, Wassily Leontief began an intensive theoretical and empirical study of these interindustry relationships. As a result primarily of his work, a new dimension has been added to economic analysis. See Wassily Leontief, *The Structure of the American Economy* (New York: Oxford University Press, 1947).

cult to grasp apart from the framework of economic accounting. As a result, even if we never use a piece of data on profits, we will be better able to manipulate the *concept* of profits if we have studied its meaning in terms of accounting for costs and revenues. Again, in the realm of macroeconomics, with a knowledge of this framework we can better understand such crucial relationships as those between savings and investment and between them and the stock of capital.

Economic accounting cuts across most of economics no matter how the economic cake is sliced. In preparation for the study of economics, it can logically assume a place in what we have referred to before as "science-readiness." Then, the simple accounts of individuals and families can be used to illustrate the important categories of stocks and flows, the equalities and the identities. Later, more detailed accounts together with the introduction of new accounts is appropriate. Finally, there are the sectoral accounts and their consolidation.

We return for a final look at a slightly more full-blown diagram of economic activity in Figure 8.3. Two major additions have been made to earlier depictions—arrows to represent the flows of money spending and "outside" boundary conditions (limitations).

The flows of income spending were discussed in the macro chapter where the whole economy was represented. Besides the income flows for business and the economy, two alternative flows were the subject of the section immediately above: input-output and cash flows. All of these are what the arrows now symbolize.

The boundary conditions or limitations have been touched upon at several points and may now be briefly illustrated in summary fashion. There are political-legal limitations that affect economic activity and therefore economic analysis: minimum wage laws that establish floors under certain wages are clearly something given to economic analysis, not something adequately explained by that analysis. Again, it may be more the politics of patronage that decides who gets a government contract than it is the economics of contracting.

It is largely because of physical-technological limitations that neither the United States nor Russia had landed a man on the moon by the mid-nineteen-sixties. The economics of the space

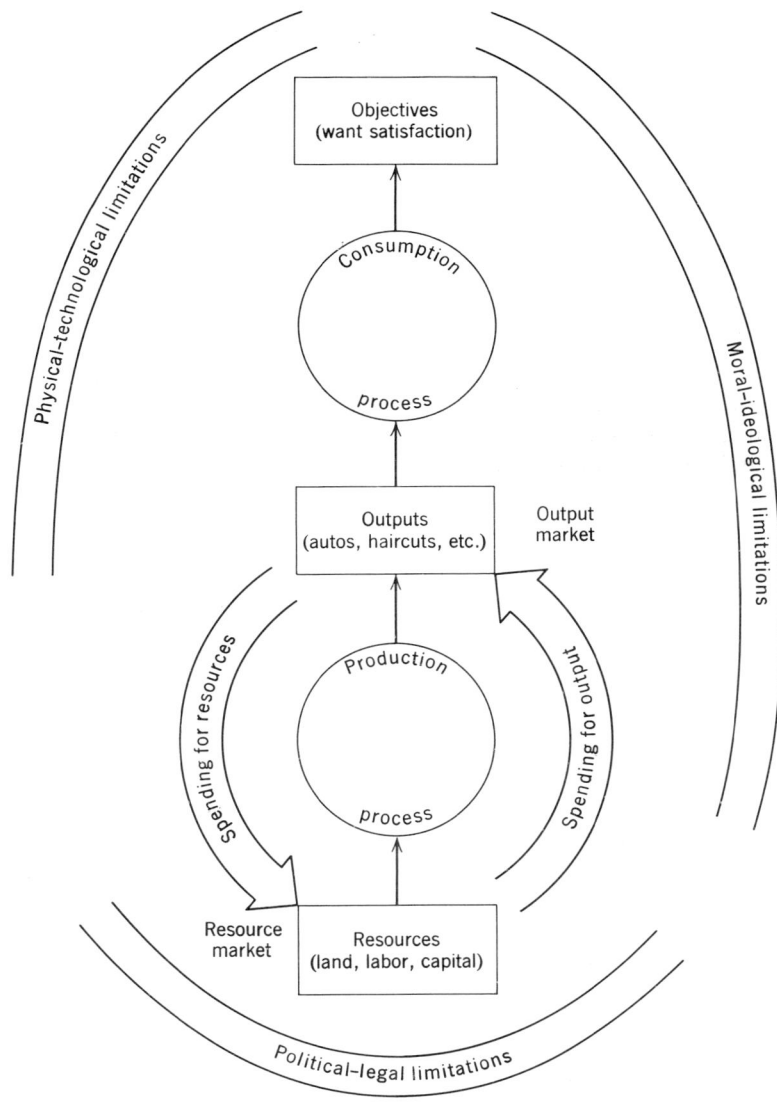

Fig. 8.3 Economic activity and its boundaries.

efforts is not to be slighted. But more overriding would appear to be such physical laws as those demanding satellite velocities of 18,000 miles an hour—and the technological problems of building the rockets and guidance systems to cope with those physical laws.

The moral-ideological constraints appear in many forms: dietary prohibitions among religions, customs affecting dress and manners, and the commitment of American military resources around the globe—all of these generally require more by way of explanation than economics has to offer.

We must be careful, however, not to turn the operation of these limitations around. For in explaining economic *consequences*, rather than chief causes, economics has a good deal to say about all of these matters. Economics has important analysis to convey on the consequences of wage laws, patronage, space probes, and the use of resources in the service of moral and ideological commitment.

The brief observations of this chapter are intended solely as a guide to the understanding of economics. We have dealt with some of the themes that bear on the ordering of economic inquiry without trying to do justice to the rich content underlying those themes. Our remarks have been largely suggestive of further lines of study that the reader may wish to pursue. Since the writing here, as elsewhere in these pages, has been aimed at questions I know are asked by those concerned with economic education, I hope I may have hit the target a few times for others with a similar curiosity.

In the next and concluding chapter of this book we return to questions of rationale for all that has gone before, questions partially dealt with at several points already. What are the distinctive aims of instruction in economics? What claims to our attention does it have different from the claims of other studies? Do the traditional educational criteria of usefulness, pleasure, and "intellectual liberation" suffice to set economics apart from other fields of inquiry? Is economic cognition, the knowledge and skills of economics, the total of economic learning? Or is there something to be said for the quality of experience that economic learning should be? A beginning at answers to these questions carries us into what educators have called the "affective domain," the large area of human sensibilities.

QUESTIONS

VALUE

Each of the following questions poses two alternatives. Circle the alternative you prefer or, if you feel neither is good, draw a line through both of them.
1. Which is more valuable, wheat or diamonds?
2. Which costs more:
    a. Hot dogs or sirloin steak?
    b. Stocks or bonds?
    c. Shoes or milk?
3. Which is more efficient:
    a. A bulldozer or a shovel?
    b. An electronic computer or an adding machine?
    c. An electronic computer or a birdbath?
4. Which would you prefer to use in order to plant three tulips in your flower garden:

    A bulldozer or a shovel?
5. Which would you prefer to use in order to figure out the costs of buying three tulips and a shovel:

    An electronic computer or an adding machine?
6. Which would you prefer to use in order to beautify your flower garden:

    An electronic computer or a birdbath?

ANSWERS

VALUE

1. It is not possible to say that one thing is more valuable than another unless units are specified. A carload of wheat is more valuable (costs more, sells for more money) than the diamond used on the end of a phonograph needle but, on the contrary, a bushel of wheat is less valuable than a 10-carat diamond. The question, then, is designed to bring out the fact that you have to specify units.
2. Of the three things listed, none can be said to cost more for the same reason given above, that is, while we think of sirloin steak as more costly than hot dogs, we cannot say which costs more until we say how much of each is to be purchased. The other items—stocks or

bonds, shoes or milk—bring out an additional dimension in comparison, namely, the time dimension. If by "cost more" we mean how much an average person spends in a year on a given commodity, then any one of these could be more costly than the other. This is particularly clear in the case of shoes or milk. The average milk drinker probably spends much more on milk than on shoes in the course of a year unless his feet are growing rapidly.

3. Like the two preceding questions, sense can only be made of these comparisons if each is related to a particular standard. In the case of the instruments of production listed in this question, one cannot say which is more efficient without knowing what is the task at hand to be performed. The necessity for having a purpose or task is brought out in the questions that follow.

4. Even without having cost data available, I imagine that with modern technology, a bulldozer is to be preferred if one is digging a Panama Canal, but a shovel is better for planting tulips.

5. Similarly, an electronic computer is a more efficient instrument for calculating the orbital path of a satellite, but an adding machine is better for adding a few simple items together.

6. Again, an electronic computer is not a very good decoration for the flower garden; a birdbath is preferable.

While some of these questions and their answers may seem facetious, the fact is that many people tend to think of certain resources as having inherent advantages over others. This is almost never the case.

In recapitulation, the economic responses are: 1, neither; 2a, b, and c: neither; 3a, b, and c: neither; 4, shovel; 5, an adding machine; 6, a birdbath.

Economists agree with the preceding answers with one curious exception, namely, 2a, where they said sirloin steak costs more than hot dogs. Here are the votes of the majority:

1. 64 percent said neither is more valuable.
2. a. 56 percent said sirloin steak costs more.
   b. 91 percent said neither costs more.
   c. 72 percent said neither costs more.
3. With little variation, about 84 percent said none is more efficient.
4. 97 percent preferred a shovel.
5. 94 percent preferred an adding machine.
6. 100 percent preferred a birdbath.

CHAPTER

9

The Aims of Economics

WHAT should be the aim of instruction in economics?

Simply put, the aim is to convey the knowledge and skills of the economist. Up to now, our attention has been devoted almost wholly to this knowledge and those skills. We have also included knowledge of the misconceptions that plague the science.

But, why should this information be taught and learned?

Part of the answer to this crucial question of why was dealt with briefly in a discussion of the achievements of modern economics where a few of the services of the discipline to social policy were mentioned. If it is important to understand a subject whose teachings vitally affect major aspects of our lives, then it is important to know something about economics. For a democracy where an informed citizenry has a voice in the conduct of affairs, the point is compelling.

But can't the same claims be made about scores of other subjects—that they have shaped social policy and have vitally affected our lives? Yes, such claims can well be made. And in this weighing of claims of enlightenment, economics has but two bases on which to demand more attention. One, that of all the social sciences, economics has been better codified into a set of principles and, two, that it has been longer neglected than most sciences in the curricula of the schools.

Let us look at three criteria that seem widely accepted for sifting out what students may profitably learn. These criteria are utility, pleasure, and emancipation. While there is overlapping, the ideas are that people study for the practical value of what they learn, for the (less obviously practical) pleasure of study, and for the (less obviously pleasurable) emanicipation of their intellects.

UTILITY, PLEASURE, AND EMANCIPATION

Is economics useful to society? Of course it is. But so is virtually every other study common to the curricula of schools, universities, and courses in adult education. The mating habits of the drosophila fruit fly, a seemingly esoteric thing to study, have provided some of the most useful genetic knowledge known to biologists. Nothing socially useful in a general sense is peculiar to economic inquiry.

Is economics useful to the individual? Of course it is. And so is almost every scrap of knowledge both when that knowledge is systematically organized and when it exists only in bits and pieces. The study of ancient languages, of Sanskrit, for example, is the most useful thing imaginable to one who seeks to understand certain venerable texts. Lest this seeking be read here as a backhanded criticism, I should state explicitly my firm belief that the study of languages, old and new, is every bit as useful as the study of any science or social science. The criterion of usefulness has too long been a false criterion for those critics of some branch of learning for which they happened to have no use. Unless it is most carefully explained, the standard of usefulness is a conceited and empty escutcheon.

Some would say that through their elected representatives, the people of the U. S. have developed a clear and purposeful definition of usefulness. Specifically, in the "panic" that followed the launching of Sputnik by the Soviet Union in 1957, usefulness came to mean serving to lessen the apparent scientific and technological gap between America and Communist Russia. But educators remained free to reject the accuracy of official estimates of the "gap" and to question, as well, the massive, crash methods designed to overcome it. In any case, the priorities of education cannot be based upon the fashions of a decade.

There may be nothing logically wrong with society's declaration that certain studies ought to be pursued in the national interest. Yet, it is equally true that such a declaration gives at best a transient sanction to those studies and in no way elevates their claim to persistent distinction. Who knows what society or even a state legislature will declare tomorrow as essential to the preservation of our way of life?

If general usefulness fails as a guide to identifying the virtues of given areas of study, what other criteria may justify us? One that comes readily to mind is pleasure. Is not economics a pleasant thing to study? Of course it is for many people, but immediately we recall the historian whose life proves to us that historical study is also pleasurable; the biochemist whose life proves the pleasure he enjoys; and so it goes. We are at the same place where usefulness left us.

Special relevance is a kind of usefulness that might seem to lend to economics a special cogency. Surely we are all victors over, or victims of, economic forces which we need to know. Our getting and spending require our attention to the cash nexus. Does it not best serve our motives for money, power, and prestige to study the economic system that chiefly apportions these values among us? The answer is, maybe so. Yet who would seriously argue that what Americans need most to know is how to acquire this world's goods? What is it that we lack which a study of economics will provide? It is certainly not a lack of knowledge of how to generate the goods and services that comprise national income.

What about the emancipation that learning brings? There are educators who claim that the purpose of liberating the human mind provides a criterion of essential study. This notion is founded in part upon the concept of Renaissance Man emerging from the static, feudal order into a world ripe for discovery and mastery, a world no longer explained and ordered by traditional dogma but one subject to the mind and will of man.

The modern university's interpretation of this humane, emancipating curriculum stems largely from professors in the liberal arts. The liberal curriculum now includes academic studies old and new. At our institutions of higher learning, the interest and competence of the faculties determine the mixture of subject matters that are called liberal but usually the list runs something like this, with semester hours assigned as requirements for undergraduate college students: English (6 hours), foreign language (12 hours), laboratory science (6 hours), mathematics (3 hours), social science (6 hours), art and music (6 hours), history (6 hours). That these requirements for the liberally educated student are of enormous importance to the professor is attested to by the fact that many faculty members spend more time debating this aspect of the college curriculum than any other. The strongest claim to preferment a professor can advance may be the hours of study a student must devote to his particular discipline. The greatest remonstrance a faculty can deliver to a professor is the elimination of the requirement that students study in "his" field.

Now, besides the politics of academic life and the favorable employment and salary effects that flow to certain professors from requiring that students must be captives in their classes, what does the liberal arts criterion suggest about the hierarchy of essential inquiry? It appears to suggest that certain *qualities of the mind* will likely develop from (forced) exposure to certain disciplined studies. What qualities? Probably sensitivities to intellectual achievements that have shaped civilization—achievements in science, art, literature, and philosophy. Yet if we were to focus our attention upon the exemplars of excellent mind rather than upon the history to which those exemplars contributed, we might find a very different kind of learning would serve the aims of liberal arts. Specifically, we might ask, "Do we wish to develop in students those qualities of mind and spirit exemplified by the great minds of today and yesterday?" If the answer is yes, we may then fairly ask, "Do these great minds show an impact from the kind of study we designate as liberal arts? Did the great men of the past meet our present-day requirements for liberal arts?" I think the answer to these last two questions is, clearly, no. The great men of the past have usually failed to pass our requirements. They were not liberally educated by modern college standards. They would not be entitled to our diploma without several semesters of remedial work.

Shakespeare surely failed the acid test of a course in a laboratory science. Socrates probably knew only Greek and is thus deficient in foreign language. Sigmund Freud shows little evidence of training in mathematics; Christ may or may not have had an adequate appreciation of art and music, but he could not have been acquainted with the baroque period. And Michelangelo was certainly lacking in social sciences. Since all of these leading lights were highly educable, it might have required only a summer of study to bring them up to snuff. But as things must stand, they cannot be (posthumously) graduated without approval of a special petition to a university's Committee on Instruction.

From all of this the tentative inference is suggested: If it is the qualities of great minds that we would foster in students, the liberal arts *as currently defined* offer no assistance in identifying those qualities or in promoting their development.

Utility, pleasure, and emancipation do not carry the educator very far in sorting out the values of instruction in economics or in any discipline. Perhaps we should be thankful for this. For as long as there is ambiguity in educational criteria we may enjoy the mixed, decentralized education that reflects our diverse, pluralistic strengths.

THE AIMS OF ECONOMICS

We have earlier discussed economics as a particular perspective upon human behavior. If it is particular, then certain things about humanity should be known primarily through this perspective. Skill in recognizing and analyzing this aspect of behavior should be a peculiar virtue of the study of economics.

There are, I think, three qualities of the mind that the study of economics is specially apt to contribute to. Briefly stated, these are qualities of style, reasoned choice, and historical insight.

These qualities, it will be seen, all derive from the analysis of alternatives that is the core of economic reasoning.

Style. Broadly conceived, economics is the analysis of the efficient attainment of objectives, the reaching of goals without needless bother, wasted effort, and circuitous meandering. Such neat, deft execution of tasks is a style of operation reflecting a quality of mind. Alfred North Whitehead calls this sense of style "the most austere of all mental qualities . . . the ultimate morality of the mind":

> It is an aesthetic sense, based on admiration for the direct attainment of a foreseen end, simply and without waste. Style in art, style in literature, style in science, style in logic, style in practical execution have fundamentally the same aesthetic qualities, namely, attainment and restraint. . . .
>
> Style, in its finest sense, is the last acquirement of the educated mind; it is also the most useful. It pervades the whole being. The administrator with a sense for style hates waste, the engineer with a sense for style economizes his material, the artisan with a sense for style prefers good work. Style is the ultimate morality of the mind.*

No one can contend, of course, that with the study of economics comes style and without the study comes a lack of style. Yet it is the province of economic analysis—shared with few other studies—wherein alternative courses of action are weighed and the optimal route chosen. Ideally, economic insight should lead to no mincing of words, thoughts, and deeds. While we should admit that economists have not always shown the world the best examples of this "ultimate morality of the mind," we may believe that it is in spite of their formal, disciplined training and not because of it.

The matter of style as defined by Whitehead needs no further explanation than that given in the quotation above. For more detail of what is meant, we may refer to some of the attempts in the present writing to show how the economic and economical analysis of problems may be optimally attained although there is no pretending that this writing shows splendid style! Once again we may state that, for whatever process one seeks a good solution among viable alternatives, an explicit governing criterion

---

* *The Aims of Education* (New York: The Macmillan Company, 1929), p. 24.

of performance is essential. This brings us to the second quality of thinking that economic study may advantageously promote, namely, the quality of reasoned choice.

Reasoned Choice. Economics is the study of the consequences of choice. In a large, formal sense, there is no specific, necessary *content* of the alternatives from among which choice is to be made. Therefore, in this formal sense, there is vast applicability for the knowledge and skills learned through the study of economics.

As a more practical matter, however, the choices that are best illuminated are those concerned with the generally measurable phenomena of the market and of business. There, economics shows its highest forms of technical excellence. All of the preceding pages are meant to convey the meaning and importance of this excellence. This is the most obvious special claim that the discipline can stake out. We need not repeat here the contributions to social policy that were spelled out in Chapter 3, nor the various illustrations of subsequent pages that applied economic analysis to the problems of individuals and of businesses. It may suffice to say that since virtually all people are producers and consumers, earners and spenders, they will generally find an analysis of their participation in economic affairs a worthwhile inquiry. Unlike *general*, social, and individual usefulness (values we may safely ascribe to all serious studies), the study of economics has particular use in these matters of reasoned choice.

There is another value to economic study that has only recently attracted attention, a value not yet fully enough understood for us to be certain of its importance. This value arises from the connections between economic scarcity and questions of morality. This matter lies right at the perimeter of known economic and philosophic knowledge but seems of potential importance and, therefore, worth the risk of a little space in these pages.*

Behavior that we term moral generally means a "right" choice of conduct, what we call immoral means a "wrong" choice of conduct. Right and wrong are, of course, derived from some moral system. If a person steals from another, we say he acted

---

* In what follows in this section, I have relied heavily upon Vivian Charles Walsh, *Scarcity and Evil* (Englewood Cliffs, N. J.: Prentice-Hall, 1961).

immorally. We must assume the person had some choice in the way he acted since, if he was forced to misbehave in this way—perhaps because someone threatened his life—then we should recognize that he had no choice and exonerate him.

It is easy enough in such a case to say of a person that his stealing does not show a wrong or immoral choice of conduct when we know he performed as he did in order to preserve his life. But how often are we able to perceive so clearly the pressure of an "outside" influence? What about other kinds of pressure that bear upon ethical conduct?

The attainment of ethically or morally approved conduct depends on the availability of the necessary means. Without adequate means, we cannot be sure of the moral adequacy of the conduct. Walsh gives the following situation as showing the way in which moral behavior depends upon essential means:

> . . . a doctor has failed to give his patient the necessary treatment, but . . . this was only because they were at sea together in a small yacht without medical supplies. . . . (Because we recognize the doctor's inability to act correctly without the essential means, we do not blame him. Rather, we make an economic statement) . . . the doctor was prevented from curing his patient by the scarcity of certain required means.*

Like our example of a person who steals under dire threat, here, too, the doctor is limited in his choice of conduct—but this time it is the absence of necessary means that constrains his choice. It is readily apparent that we are only a few short steps from moral problems of a much more difficult kind. The greater difficulty arises as soon as we consider an instance where evaluating the adequacy of the means is not a simple matter.

As illustrations of the difficulty of finding the adequacy of the means to moral conduct, imagine trying to figure out the morally correct behavior in the following questions. In each case you might ask, "How adequate are the means at hand to the attainment of morally correct behavior?" A German citizen, living under the Nazi regime, seeks to act consistently with his religious beliefs. A President of the United States ponders the question of dropping an atomic bomb on Hiroshima. An American soldier,

---

* *Ibid.*, pp. 7-8.

captured by the Chinese during the Korean War, is "asked" to sign statements injurious to his country's diplomatic and military efforts.

If we accept the notion that scarcity of means, in the economic sense, serves as an important limitation upon the choice of moral conduct, then we may agree with Walsh that "an analysis which succeeds in showing a close connection between the concept of scarcity and some of the key concepts of ethics must raise questions as to the status, the importance, of the economic aspect of experience."*

As far as I know, no one has worked out the connection between economics and ethics. Certainly these few pages are but a mere interpretation of one philosopher's imaginative speculation. Yet it seems likely that a science whose specialty is the implications of choice should have a uniquely interesting connection with any ethical system wherein right conduct depends upon reasoned choice among alternatives.

We conclude this section by adding a historical and psychological note to our discussion of behavior that is approved or highly valued.

The values of a society persist, says Erikson,** because they become essential to a person's sense of identity, his sanity, and his efficiency. Moreover, to persist they must work "economically, psychologically, and spiritually." But, especially in a rapidly changing society, virtues that used to serve the aims of both individuals and society may cease to serve and may, indeed, become encumbrances and vices. Like the salmon that attempts to spawn in waters now too polluted to sustain the lives of newly hatched fish, so man suffers the economic burden of outworn social custom, preserving a former virtue that has now become a vice: the nomadic Indian plainsman who customarily gives away what little he has even while a ward of the state, subsisting on the government's dole; the citizen who hoards his money in a mattress because of his experience with the unsound banks of thirty years ago. As Erikson points out:

---

* *Ibid.*, p. 106.
** Erik Erikson, *Childhood and Society* (New York: W. W. Norton & Company, Inc., 1953), p. 138.

But necessities change more rapidly than true virtues, and it is one of the most paradoxical problems of human evolution that virtues which were originally designed to safeguard an individual's or group's self-preservation become rigid under the pressure of anachronistic fears of extinction and thus can render a people unable to adapt to changed necessities. In fact, such relics of old virtues become stubborn and yet elusive obstacles to re-education. For, once deprived of their overall economic meaning and universal observance, they fall apart. . . . In the end the administrator and teacher cannot possibly know when they are dealing with an old virtue, when with a new vice.*

The study of economics has special merit in helping to draw distinctions between customs that remain enlivened by virtuous economic function and customs, robbed of their function, that have become vices.

Historical Insight. Leading historians have emphasized that history is most concerned with the particular, the concrete, the unique in man's past behavior.** Economics, on the other hand, especially in its theoretical cast, is occupied with the general, the abstract, the plurality. It is not the contribution of a great man, an overwhelming idea, or a disastrous calamity that absorbs the

---

* *Ibid.*, p. 129.

** Cf. R. G. Collingwood, *The Idea of History* (New York: Oxford University Press, 1946), p. 5: "Historical thought has an object with peculiarities of its own. The past, consisting of particular events in time and space which are no longer happening, cannot be apprehended by mathematical thinking, because mathematical thinking apprehends objects that have no special location in space and time, and it is just that lack of peculiar spatiotemporal location that makes them knowable. Nor can the past be apprehended by theological thinking, because the object of that kind of thinking is a single infinite object, and historical events are finite and plural. Nor by scientific thinking, because the truths which science discovers are known to be true by being found through observation and experiment exemplified in what we actually perceive, whereas the past has vanished and our ideas about it can never be verified as we verify our scientific hypotheses. Theories of knowledge designed to account for mathematical and theological and scientific knowledge thus do not touch on the special problems of historical knowledge; and if they offer themselves as complete accounts of knowledge they actually imply that historical knowledge is impossible."

Except for the contrast with theological knowledge, the entire quotation is directly suited to contrasts between economic and historical knowledge as these forms of knowledge are represented in the above discussion.

attention and shapes the mind of an economist. Rather, it is the average of values, the modal behavior, the median of response. Economics, in an important sense, is antihistorical and history is antieconomic—with economic defined as abstract and analytical. It is this antithesis that leads to the following kind of pronouncement from a philosopher of history:

> The "historical" is essentially a coherent form of existence. For the concrete in its literal sense signifies something that grows together and coheres, as opposed to the abstract, detached, dissociated, and divided. *Everything abstract is by its nature opposed to the historical.* (Emphasis added.)*

History and economics are, then, complementary forms of inquiry. Each is essential to an appreciation of the other. And the reason they are complementary to the mind is that they represent points of view that are largely antagonistic.

The antagonism may be summed up in two well-known quotations on the value of history. Santayana declared, "Those who do not remember the past are condemned to relive it." By contrast, an economic adage says, "In economics, by-gones are forever bygones." Perhaps a little illustration can clarify the nature of this conflict.

Imagine that you have just ended a day's visit to Canada and are standing at the American customs station declaring a piece of merchandise that you bought to take back home to the United States. The item in question is a bottle of perfume for which you paid five dollars in Montreal. You know that the perfume sells for ten dollars in the States. But you learn from the American customs official that you must pay a duty or tariff of seven dollars if you wish to take it home. The question is, should you now pay an additional seven dollars (having already paid five for the purchase in Montreal), thus raising your expenditure on the perfume to twelve dollars? Or should you let the customs official take the perfume and buy a bottle in the United States for ten dollars?

The economist would answer simply that you should pay the seven dollars duty. This is more economical than spending ten

---

* Nicholas Berdyaev, *The Meaning of History*, George Reavey, trans. (Cleveland: The World Publishing Company, 1962), p. 24.

dollars in the United States. He would emphasize that the five dollars spent in Montreal on the purchase is irrelevant to the choice at hand; the five dollars is over the dam or down the drain. You can't do anything about it and it shouldn't enter into an evaluation of the choice. Historical circumstance is extraneous, bygones are bygones.

The historian might argue quite differently. First of all, if you pay the seven dollar duty you will have spent twelve dollars on the perfume. This is two dollars more than you need to pay in the United States. Such extravagance may spoil your enjoyment of the perfume. And while the choice was expressed as spending seven dollars more now or ten dollars later, the crucial matter may be, how much later? Perhaps you cannot spare seven dollars now after living wildly in Canada while maybe ten dollars "later" does not seem like much money. Time may be the essence of the whole problem.

Of course, there is no "right" solution, and the considerations we have attributed to economist and historian may all be equally relevant. But the stress of the former upon the contemporaneous problem of choice and of the latter upon the bearing of historical circumstance may serve to symbolize their divergent ways of thinking. It is fair to say that analysis that abstracts from the flux of time has great strength potentially: it frees us from the chains of dead precedent. Yet at the same time it runs grave dangers of overlooking the crucially influential role of past circumstance in shaping the present course of events. Economics and history are each necessary antidotes to the myopia of the other.

In answer to Santayana's emphasis that ignorance of the past condemns man to repeat its errors is the equally sound psychological insight that a man who cannot forget the past may be neurotically enslaved to its remembrance. "Our hysterical patients," said Freud, "suffer from reminiscences."* At greater length he wrote:

What should we think of a Londoner who paused today in deep melancholy before the memorial of Queen Eleanor's funeral instead of

---

* Quoted by Rieff. I have this quotation and the one cited next from N. O. Brown, "History," 1959 (mimeographed).

going about his business on the hurry that modern working conditions demand or instead of feeling joy over the youthful queen of his own heart? Or again, what should we think of a Londoner who shed tears before the monument which commemorates the reduction of his beloved metropolis to ashes although it has long since risen again in far greater brilliance? Yet every single hysteric and neurotic behaves like these two impractical Londoners. Not only do they remember powerful experiences of the remote past, but they still cling to them emotionally; they cannot get free of the past and for its sake, they neglect what is real and immediate.*

Psychoanalysis, like economic analysis, is a discriminating criticism of historical method; its function is the transcendence of much of history. Yet, of course, it is subject itself to an historical critique.

This section of our excursion into the peculiar virtues of economics is entitled "Historical Insight" for the very good reason that it does not presume to give preeminence to economics over the study of history. Rather, the point is simply that social analysis and large understanding require a fine balance between historical and abstractly analytical thinking.

Style, reasoned choice, and historical insight are intellectual attainments to which the study of economics can make uniquely valuable contributions. This is not to give priority to the study of economics but, rather, to try to mark its distinguishing characteristics.

QUESTIONS

TOO MUCH

Check the space before each saying, showing whether you think an economist would agree or disagree with the statement that follows.

---

* Freud, *Complete Works*, XI, pp. 16-17, quoted by Brown, Op. cit. For an analytically balanced, forward view of history by an historian, see Paul L. Ward, "Should History be Cherished? Some Doubts and Affirmations," *Social Education*, Vol. XXXI, No. 3, March 1967, pp. 188-92. For the backward view, see Mark M. Krug, "Bruner's New Social Studies: A Critique," *Ibid.*, Vol. XXX, No. 6, October 1966, pp. 400-6.

What brief comment might an economist be expected to make with respect to each?

Agree   Disagree

_____   _____   1. If at first you don't succeed, try, try, again.
                   Comment:
_____   _____   2. Whatever is worth doing at all is worth doing well.
                   Comment:
_____   _____   3. It is better to have loved in vain than never to have loved at all.
                   Comment:
_____   _____   4. Consistency is the hobgoblin of little minds.
                   Comment:
_____   _____   5. A bird in the hand is worth two in the bush.
                   Comment:

ANSWERS

TOO MUCH

I'm sure different people would place different interpretations on each of the following pieces of conventional wisdom; nevertheless, I think I can give reasonable reactions to them.

1. "If at first you don't succeed, try, try, again."
   I disagree. In the world of the economist, those things are tried that have some probability of success. If a trial fails, then costs and benefits must be reckoned anew. The statement seems to suggest that if you fail, you should try again without reckoning costs and benefits. Failures are followed by repeated trials. This is certainly not ordinary behavior nor for that matter does it seem like rational behavior. Both economics and common sense agree that after a while you should stop trying because what you are trying is too difficult to do—not "worth" doing.
2. "Whatever is worth doing at all is worth doing well." I disagree. Like the preceding statement, this aphorism has too much an all-or-none quality about it. The human condition with which economic

analysis is conformable suggests a more realistic view of human behavior than is implied by the prescription. It makes no sense for a person who takes up the game of bridge to feel he should not play at all if he does not play well. Of course, everything appears to hinge on how we define "doing well." But the opposite of the statement would seem to be nearer to the truth, namely, "Of all the things we do, only a few are worth our developing much expertise or skill."

3. "It is better to have loved in vain than never to have loved at all." I must confess it is not easy to develop a comment on this little piece of advice except by straining some combination of psychology and economics. To advance immediately a philosophical position, I might simply say that if man has a capacity to love, it would seem a shame not to use it. Therefore, this statement is agreeable—to me, at least.

4. "Consistency is the hobgoblin of little minds." I disagree.
This is, in fact, a misquotation of Emerson. The correct line should read: "A foolish consistency is the hobgoblin of little minds."
With the corrected statement, an economist or any person of scientific persuasion would be forced to agree. In these pages we have attempted to do a considerable amount of work with the idea of systems and interrelationships among components that form systems. One of the prerequisites of systematic analysis is consistency among relationships. Without consistency, one gets one or more of the following results from a piece of analysis: contradictory results, indeterminate results, or absurd results.
By a "foolish" consistency, Emerson probably meant the attempt to be governed by conflicting criteria or the attempt to be so consistent in one aspect of behavior that the sum total of behavior was wrecked.

5. "A bird in the hand is worth two in the bush." I disagree.
Common sense and economics dictate that the probability of getting two large birds from the bush may be much more highly valued than having in hand a scrawny little bird.
This statement calls to the mind of an economist the notion of investment and the rate of interest. We know that people buy $25.00 Series E War Bonds which mature several years in the future for a cash outlay of $18.75. Ignoring the mixed motives for purchasing these bonds, the fact is that a person who buys one of them is saying that $25.00—by and by—is worth at least as much as $18.75 now. In other words, as a practical matter we do value *possibilities* of possession more highly than *possessions* in many instances. As the reader would guess, this means that sometimes the economist would agree

with this statement and sometimes he would not. A clear answer depends upon the sizes of the birds and the probability of their possession. But I have given "disagree" as the answer until someone specifies the sizes and probabilities.

While a majority of the economists disagreed with every one of the adages, the majority was large in only two or three cases, numbers 2 and 4 and, perhaps, 1. This suggests that the other statements have fewer economic interpretations. (The following list is in percentages.)

Agree	Disagree	
42	58	1. If at first you don't succeed, try, try, again.
26	74	2. Whatever is worth doing at all is worth doing well.
47	53	3. It is better to have loved in vain than never to have loved at all.
40	60	4. Consistency is the hobgoblin of little minds.
44	56	5. A bird in the hand is worth two in the bush.

APPENDIX

A

DEEP

The writing of this book about economics has been aided, wittingly and unwittingly, by many people. Not all of them would agree with the interpretations I have worked out; yet the help of all must be acknowledged. Foremost are the coordinators in the major school systems with whom the Joint Council is carrying forward the Developmental Economic Education Program (DEEP) for curriculum enrichment. While these coordinators of economic education occupy key positions in their school systems, they are here identified simply as those who have labored in the special endeavor of increasing the economic understanding of thousands of school children.*

Albert Alexander, New York, New York
Joseph H. Black; Marie Edwards, Gary, Indiana
Michael B. Cannon, Granite, Utah
Phyllis Coker Shutt; Jack Carr, Chattanooga, Tennessee
Armand R. Colang, Seattle, Washington

---

* Where one coordinator has succeeded another because of changes in staff, the names of the several coordinators have been shown. The last name appearing is that of the current coordinator.

Donald Dowd, Dade County, Florida
Malcolm Dutterer, Jr.; Edward L. Biller, Baltimore, Maryland
K. O. Esping (deceased); Dorothy Simms, Downey, California
Roy Andreen; William Green; Robert Evans; Marion Faustman, Contra Costa County, California
Kopple C. Friedman; William Miller, Minneapolis, Minnesota
Charles A. Goddard, Manhasset, New York
Beryl A. Hamilton, Wichita, Kansas
Ray Hiner; C. Fred Bateman, Richmond, Virginia
Robert J. Kaczorowski; Robert J. McTigue, Chicago Archdiocese, Illinois
Eleanor R. Kambour; Carl Deyeso, Quincy, Massachusetts
John Kilgore, Des Moines, Iowa
Hugh G. Lovell, Portland, Oregon
Noel Mcguire, Little Rock, Arkansas
Jeannette B. Moon, Atlanta, Georgia
Russell Mosely; H. Mike Hartoonian, Madison, Wisconsin
Sister M. Patrice Byrne, Duluth, Minnesota
Mrs. Vincent Patrick, Tulsa, Oklahoma
Louise E. Colvert; Anthony J. Petrillo, Jefferson County, Colorado
William F. Schulze, Trenton Diocese, New Jersey
David B. Smith, Lansing, Michigan
John F. Soboslay, Pittsburgh, Pennsylvania
Norman Sorensen, Omaha, Nebraska
Werner E. Stickel, San Diego, California
Lewis C. Vinson, New Orleans, Louisiana

The consulting economists who have worked with the coordinators are exemplars of that unity of effort by schools, colleges, and universities that is essential for sound curriculum change in the social sciences.

CAROL ADAMS, *Silver Spring, Maryland*
BURVIN ALREAD, *Hendrix College, Conway, Arkansas*
WILLIAM H. BAUGHN, *University of Colorado*
JOHN L. BERTON, *University of Arkansas*
JOSEPH BLUMEL, *Portland State College*
JAMES BOBO, *Louisiana State University*
THEODORE BOYDEN, *Georgia State College*
JOHN CHISHOLM, *Louisiana State University*
JERE W. CLARK, *Southern Connecticut State College*

Donald G. Davison, *University of Iowa*
George Dawson, *New York University*
Demetrios Dertouzos, *Trenton, New Jersey*
Frank Doody, *Boston University*
Marie Edwards, *Gary, Indiana*
Matthew Gibney, *University of Maryland*
Linda Graham, *Wichita, Kansas*
John I. Griffin, *Baruch School of Business and Public Administration, New York City*
Whitney Hanks, *University of Utah*
John D. Helmberger, *College of St. Thomas, St. Paul, Minnesota*
Robert L. Hemond, *American International College, Springfield, Massachusetts*
John Hicks, *Purdue University*
J. Fred Holly, *University of Tennessee*
Richard Huber, *University of Washington*
Robert Johnson, *University of Virginia*
John Lafky, *California State College at Fullerton*
Sylvia Lane, *California State College at Fullerton*
William N. Leonard, *Hofstra University*
Robert Lyon, *Temple University*
Leonard Martin, *Loyola University*
Joseph McClintic, *San Diego State College*
Vernon Mund, *University of Washington*
Robert Nelson, *Wisconsin State University*
Bernard Newton, *Long Island University*
James Niss, *University of Illinois*
Glen Ovard, *Brigham Young University*
Elinor Pancoast, *Towson State College, Maryland*
Joseph Perry, *University of Utah*
James P. Payne, *Louisiana State University*
Everett Refior, *Wisconsin State University*
Louis J. Rodriguez, *Francis T. Nicholls College, Thibodaux, Louisiana*
Phillip Saunders, *Carnegie Institute of Technology*
Lorraine H. Scheer, *University of Tulsa*
Ewing P. Shahan, *Vanderbilt University*
Myron J. Spencer, *Northeastern University, Boston, Massachusetts*
Elroy J. Steele, *Municipal University of Omaha*
John Terry, *John Brown University, Siloam Springs, Arkansas*

NORMAN TOWNSHEND-ZELLNER, *California State College at Fullerton*
JAMES C. VADAKIN, *University of Miami*
SALVATORE VALENTINO, *Creighton University, Omaha, Nebraska*
CHARLES VENUS, *University of Arkansas*
DOUGLAS VICKERS, *University of Pennsylvania*
LEWIS E. WAGNER, *University of Iowa*
BART WESTERLAND, *University of Arkansas*
SUZANNE WIGGINS, *San Jose State College*
L. CURTISE WOOD, *Wichita State University*
KASHTEN AL YASIRI, *Wisconsin State University*

Readers who are interested in any of the exciting experimental programs going on in these school systems and assisted by the universities cited above should write to the persons mentioned or to the Joint Council on Economic Education, 1212 Avenue of the Americas, New York, New York 10036.

APPENDIX

B

Economic Knowledge (Taxonomic)

The study of a discipline may be considered as a double process. On the one hand, the person engaged in study is *storing* in his mind various kinds of *knowledge*. On the other hand, he is *developing skills* in the use of this knowledge. The distinction between these two functions of the intellect is essential to an appreciation of the ideal outcomes toward which learning strives: the storing of knowledge or information and the developing of skills in its use. While no one pretends that the distinction can always be clearly perceived, it is, nonetheless, useful to the study of education.

In this appendix, we are largely occupied with economic *knowledge*, the kinds of things that a student might store in the warehouse of his mind. In Appendix C, we shall have something to say about the *skills* a student may develop in the use of this knowledge.

Confining ourselves to the knowledge that is economics, how may we categorize the things that are to be stored in the mind? Following the taxonomy developed by Benjamin S. Bloom and his associates, we may break the economic cake into three kinds of knowledge with a few subdivisions for each.* Illustrative examples of the divisions of economic

---

* Bloom (ed.), Englehart, Furst, Hill, and Krathwohl, *Taxonomy of Educational Objectives*, Handbook I: *Cognitive Domain* (New York: Longmans, Green, and Co., 1956).

Table B.1 The Cognitive Domain: Illustrations of Knowledge (1.00) From Mathematics and Economics

	Mathematics	Economics
1.10 Knowledge of specifics		
1.11 Knowledge of terminology	"Σ" means summation.	Money supply means currency, coins and demand deposits.
1.12 Knowledge of specific facts	$\Pi = 3.14159$ (apx.)	The national debt in the U.S. was about $300 billion in 1965.
1.20 Knowledge of ways and means of dealing with specifics		
1.21 Knowledge of conventions	$3! = 3 \times 2 \times 1$ Three factorial (3!) means the product of three times two times one.	By conventional usage, AC symbolizes average cost of production.
1.22 Knowledge of trends and sequences	The series: $1/2 + 1/4 + 1/8 + 1/16 \ldots + 1/2^n$ converges upon a final term of zero as n becomes infinite; the series has a finite value approaching one.	Business downturns often begin with declines in orders for durable goods; declines in industrial production and in national income follow.
1.23 Knowledge of classification and categories	Systems of equations like $X + Y = 2$ and $X - Y = 0$ belong to a class called linear algebra.	Capital (man-made instruments of production) is a major category of the factors of production.
1.24 Knowledge of criteria	Two equations must satisfy the criterion of consistency if they are to be solved simultaneously. ($X + Y = 2$ and $X + Y = 7$ are inconsistent.)	"Maximum profits" is (assumed to be) the criterion for efficient operation of a business firm.
1.25 Knowledge of methodology	Logarithms are an efficient device for solving multiplicative and exponential functions.	A test of an optimal solution is equality at the margin (cf. above, pp. 39 ff.).
1.30 Knowledge of the universals and abstractions in a field		

Table B.1 *Continued*

	Mathematics	Economics
1.31 Knowledge of principles and generalizations	The commutative principle asserts that the order in which a sum is arrived at does not affect the sum, $(1 + 2 = 2 + 1)$	The principle of Diminishing Returns. (cf. above, pp. 37-38).
1.32 Knowledge of theories and structures	The theory of numbers	Schumpeter's (or Marx's) theory of capitalist development.

knowledge appear in Table B.1. (For comparative purposes, an illustrative listing appears also for mathematics.) By briefly going over this tabular listing we shall be able to see how economic knowledge fits into a general classifying scheme based on educational research. Moreover, by noticing what has been emphasized and what has been just touched upon, we shall see what is important in economics—according to the predilections of the present author.

The first of three general headings of knowledge is Knowledge of Specifics (1.10), subdivided into knowledge of terminology (1.11) and of specific facts (1.12). The table illustrates economic terminology by stating that when economists refer to the money supply they mean, roughly, currency (paper money), coins, and demand deposits (checking account balances). Anyone who is preparing to do even casual reading in the field will find it essential to learn the definition of the money supply. Equally important are definitions of such basic terms as income, production, and consumption. Enormous economies are achieved in learning through the use of widely standardized expressions. Of course, the number of "essential" terms is smaller for primary school children than for students in junior and senior high school. Moreover, it would always seem wise to be sure that only functionally essential definitions be committed to memory and that importance be attached to the *meaning* of a term as well as to the ability to recall its name. The ability to recite a set of definitions demonstrates a good memory for specifics, but little more.

About the same comments can be made about the other subdivision of Knowledge of Specifics, which is knowledge of specific facts (1.12). It is a specific fact of economic consequence that Adam Smith published his book, *The Wealth of Nations*, in 1776. If general history or the history of economic thought is the theme of a course of study, then this specific fact may be deemed valuable. From the point of view of economic science, however, specific facts have only a small place. How much prices have risen since World War II, how many federal reserve districts there are—these scraps of specific knowledge are of little avail in understanding the discipline. Moreover, if anyone wishes to look up a fact, there is an abundance of reference books available. It is skill in getting relevant facts, not their memorization, that is worthwhile. Most of this kind of knowledge, therefore, has been left out of the discussion in this book.

The second of the three major divisions of knowledge holds greater interest for us: Knowledge of Ways and Means of Dealing with Specifics (1.20). The first of the five subdivisions of this ways-and-means category is knowledge of conventions (1.21). Like knowledge of terminology, knowledge of conventions can be of immense value, especially to advanced practitioners of economics. How convenient for both reader and writer alike to know that when an economist speaks of AC, he usually means the average cost of production. Yet the convenience or economy made possible through filling the mind with economic conventions is generally not great for beginning students.

Knowledge of trends and sequences (1.22) gathers together the historical dimension of a discipline. You will notice that for an illustration from mathematics we have fabricated the case of a numerical series which, when suitably arrayed, exhibits a "trend." It might have been preferable to cite a trend in the historical development of mathematics, say, the theory of calculus from Newton's time to the present. But my ignorance of mathematics coupled with a lack of desire to stress here the historical angle argue against the attempt. By extension, I should apply similar reasoning to the importance of knowledge of trends and sequences in economics. It is true that to explain any dynamic phenomena in economics, such knowledge is absolutely necessary. But to understand economic analysis itself, no such knowledge is required. The last chapter of this book deals in part with the interesting connections between the economic and the historical perspectives on human behavior.

Knowledge of classifications and categories (1.23) contains much more that is requisite to understanding economics. At a fairly high level of abstraction, we have classified or categorized economics into five major parts: resources, production, outputs, consumption, and want satisfaction. Again, we have classified each of these five into various components (pp. 48 to 49). The relationships that bind the parts into a system that permits systematic analysis have also been categorized (pp. 48 to 50). Of all the economic knowledge that might be stored in the mind of a student of the discipline, this is probably the most important.

Knowledge of criteria (1.24) in economics could be expanded beyond what little we have done with it in our discussion. Most vital to our inquiry is the general criterion developed for a satisfactory solution to economic problems (pp. 39 to 45). This was roughly stated as getting the maximum satisfaction of objectives through the use of given resources. General illustrations served to exemplify the use of this criterion. The illustration in the table gives the maximization of profits as a criterion of performance for a business firm. Under certain circumstances, the minimization of costs for the achievement of stated objectives leads to a perfectly analogous solution of problems as does the maximization of achievement. All of this, carefully interpreted, is central to an understanding of economics.

Knowledge of methodology (1.25) is the last of the five subdivisions of the ways-and-means category of knowledge. Here it is obvious that a definition of methodology is crucial and, at best, this is a slippery business. If by *method* we mean the peculiar *perspective* on human behavior that is economics, then, indeed, economics has (and is) a method. But short of this all-out position, no special methods distinguish the discipline. And I think the same may be said of all the social sciences. They are all deductive and inductive, they all gather information in much the same ways, and these ways have generally had antecedents in the natural sciences. They all test hypotheses in the same manner and draw, as occasion warrants, upon a vast and common pool of statistical and mathematical techniques. There is nothing like the particle accelerator of nuclear physics, the centrifuge of chemistry, and the couch of psychoanalysis—nothing like these to set the social sciences apart from other sciences nor economics from the other social sciences.

Thus, except in the general way in which economics organizes its special perspective upon human behavior, it has no distinctive methods. There are no laboratories, no economic spectroscopes, no techniques of analysis that are not also used in other areas of inquiry.

We come to the third and last general division of knowledge, Knowledge of the Universals and Abstractions in a Field (1.30), subdivided into two parts: knowledge of principles and generalizations (1.31) and knowledge of theories and structures (1.32).

The first of these subdivisions, knowledge of principles, houses much that is important to an understanding of economics. The table cites the law of diminishing returns as an example. But this example can be multiplied even from the previous brief discussions. Included as major principles are: the principle of scarcity and the related idea of opportunity cost; the economizing principle and the criterion of optimality; the relationships of substitution among factors of production and among outputs in consumption. All of these are the mortar that binds the components of economic analysis into a coherent body of thought.

The second of the subdivisions, knowledge of theories and structures, is illustrated in the table by theories of capitalist development. Probably the Marxian dialectic of antagonistic social classes is as commonly known a variety of such theories as we could cite.* The importance of this kind of general theory looms large in our understanding of the bearing of economic forces upon social development. Yet, to the extent that our attention is focused upon the central core of economic analysis as perceived and taught in the early years of education, general theories must play a relatively minor role. That is, until the elements of a discipline have been comprehended, the working of these elements into major explanations of social change is premature.

Now, when are "the early years of education" that should precede the study of major theoretical explanations of social phenomena? This, of course, depends upon the content and method of instruction. If students in junior high school have systematically explored the nature of economic inquiry, they may in high school be ready to embark upon the adventure of these larger hypotheses; if the groundwork is laid early in high school, the hypotheses are suitably treated at the senior high school level. All one can say about existing practicalities is that most students are not ready until their second or third year in college simply because most students have had little or no preparation before that time.

To summarize our brief discussion of economic knowledge:

Like other knowledge, the fund of information about economics is something we may consider as suitable for storage in the mind. (Skill in the *use* of this knowledge is another matter.) Among the categories of knowledge most essential to a mastery of the subject are:

---

* I should not want to argue with a sociologist that the Marxian theory belongs more properly to sociology. Indeed, the economic foundation of the theory is quite shaky.

Appendix B   159

knowledge of terminology (1.11)
knowledge of classification or categories (1.23)
knowledge of criteria (1.24)
knowledge of principles and generalizations (1.31)

It is these which comprise the knowledge structure of the discipline.

Other categories of knowledge may be important to understanding a special problem or a particular topic in economics—say, money and banking—but they do not form the basis of the subject. Among these less important kinds of knowledge are knowledge of specific facts, conventions, trends and sequences, methodology, and theories and structures.

This brief excursion into a formal method of organizing information should suggest ways for the transmission of economic knowledge. Surely the teaching and learning of economics can be better advanced if the one discipline is seen within the larger framework of many disciplines.

APPENDIX

C

Economic Skills (Taxonomic)

Appendix B entitled "Economic Knowledge" discussed the different kinds of knowledge that constitute the body of economics. Delineating the subject according to the taxonomy of Bloom and his associates, we noted that there was knowledge of conventions and terminology, of criteria, and so forth. The purpose of that classification was conveniently thought of as setting up storage bins in the warehouse of the mind. The student of economics requires this fund of knowledge in order to draw upon items useful to the understanding and solution of economic problems. But it is not enough to place knowledge in the mind. After all, the point of having knowledge is to put it to some use. And skill in the *use* of knowledge is a different matter from its mere possession. While the distinction is sometimes difficult to make and may often involve epistemological riddles, there is a distinction between knowledge and its use, between an encyclopedic and an agile mind, between data in a computer and a program for the execution of tasks.

In this section I shall attempt a sortie into the taxonomy of skills or abilities in the use of economic knowledge. There will be only an attempt to illustrate from the preceding discussion of the light bulb case (Chapter 6) a few of the ways in which economic knowledge is put in the service of inquiry. The treatment that follows is brief and the matters dealt with novel in the sense that the taxonomy is of recent origin and few attempts have been made to relate it to a social science. Because it is new to me and, probably, to the reader, the steps to be taken in the remaining paragraphs of this section may be set down in summary fashion:

1. There is a body of economic knowledge, some of whose features were traced in Chapter 3. Of greatest immediate consequence is the fivefold scheme for describing economic activity.

2. There are certain specific facts known about the Detroit Edison Company and its "free" light bulb policy.

3. To answer questions about the policy requires skills in combining economic knowledge with specific facts.

4. Examples of these skills are examples of the categories of intellectual abilities that make up the *modus operandi* of economic science.

In trying to answer the question, who pays for the "free" light bulbs that Detroit Edison provides its customers, we brought to bear, as a system, the fivefold division of economic activity—resources, production, consumption, outputs, and objectives; the price and substitution relationships that bind the parts into a system; and the notion of profit-maximizing efficiency for the company and satisfaction-maximizing efficiency for consumers.

Next, a few specific facts about the Detroit Edison Company were assembled: the price of light bulbs to the company and to customers, at retail; the way the cost of bulbs was treated by the Public Service Commission; and the taxation of profits. (Of course, skill in deciding what facts are relevant and how they are relevant is necessarily assumed.)

Now what intellectual abilities or skills did we need to bring to bear upon our knowledge in order to answer the question: Who pays for the light bulbs? An outline of the kinds of abilities requisite to this task is shown in Table C.1. Cognitive Domain—Intellectual Abilities and Skills.* There we see five kinds of skills, each one, except the

---

* Benjamin S. Bloom, David R. Krathwohl, and Bertram B. Masa, *Taxonomy of Educational Objectives: The Classification of Educational Goals, Handbook I: Cognitive Domain* (New York: David McKay Company, Inc., 1956).

Table C.1 Cognitive Domain: Intellectual Abilities and Skills

Taxonomic Category	Illustrative Example From Chapter 6
2.00 Comprehension	
2.10 Translation	By output of the Detroit Edison Company is meant kilowatt hours of electricity.
2.20 Interpretation	The cost of light bulbs to the Company is interpreted to mean a variable expense of production.
2.30 Extrapolation	
3.00 Application	The fivefold scheme of economic activity is a symbolic representation applied to the Company.
4.00 Analysis	
4.10 Analysis of elements	It is assumed that under specified conditions, cost reductions will lead to lower prices to consumers.
4.20 Analysis of relationships	Average costs of production decline with increases in the level of production.
4.30 Analysis of organizational principles	Technological change is assumed to be absent from the industry.
5.00 Synthesis	
5.10 Production of a unique communication	The writing of such a communication as Chapter 6, "Free Light Bulbs?" is the production of a unique communication.
5.20 Production of a plan or proposed set of operations	
5.30 Derivation of a set of abstract relations	
6.00 Evaluation	
6.10 Judgments in terms of internal evidence	Are the conclusions drawn consistent with the internal logic and facts of the analysis?
6.20 Judgments in terms of external criteria	Are the conclusions drawn consistent with external criteria?

second, broken down into various components. We require, in order to analyze the problem before us, comprehension (2.00); application (3.00); analysis (4.00); synthesis (5.00); and evaluation (6.00). These five kinds of ability may briefly be considered in the order in which they appear

APPENDIX C 163

in that table, although, of course, in tackling a problem one would hardly expect to crimp his imagination by rigid adherence to any such order of steps.

One thing that had to be done is this: the economic knowledge had to be *translated* (2.10) into the context of the operation of a public utility. This required, for example, that the economic category output be signified by kilowatt hours of electricity and the complementary "output," light bulbs. The resources used in the productive process were identified as the services of labor, the property of stockholders and others, and the materials absorbed by the industry. Particular emphasis was placed upon the light bulbs purchased by Detroit Edison. Along with this translation of economic knowledge and specific fact into a concrete situation, an *interpretation* (2.20) was required of the facts that have been listed above. To give a single instance of the matter of interpretation, we note that when the cost of light bulbs is said to be part of the ordinary expense of doing business, we must interpret this as an addition to the cost of running the business, a cost which will fluctuate with the amount of electricity consumed by the public and, more importantly, a cost which the Public Service Commission will allow before the calculation of profit. It obviously makes a very great difference to a company whether or not a cost is allowed by a regulatory authority. If an expense is *not* allowed, then it will be counted a part of profits and the tax upon the company will be greater.

A clearer example of translation and interpretation could be developed by expressing the behavior of the company in algebraic equations which, taken together, would form a system describing the operation of the utility. Since mathematics itself is a language, this instance of translation would be much clearer than those cited in the preceding paragraphs. Obviously, each instance of translation requires interpretation.

The best example of application (3.00) is the use of the fivefold classification of economic activity to represent and describe the operation of the Detroit Edison Company. The general five-part scheme was applied directly to a particular business firm, each part being identified with some aspect of the firm. This kind of representation is model building and is similar, in the natural sciences, to wind tunnels for testing airplane designs, to architectural models of buildings, and to prototypes in all kinds of research. It is largely a matter of examining the operation of this model that constitutes the remainder of our discussion of intellectual abilities in the cognitive domain.

To illustrate the ingredients of analysis (4.00), we may refer to some of the hypotheses that were given about the cost of the policy. An assumption attached to the first hypothesis was to the effect that if consumers were paying for the bulbs, then abandoning the policy would mean that electric charges to consumers would drop by an amount equal to the cost of the bulbs (analysis of elements, 4.10). A further examination of this hypothesis revealed that, if the policy had so stimulated consumption of electricity that economies of scale had led to reduced average costs of production, then abandoning the policy would not result in so large a drop in consumers' electric bills (analysis of relationships, 4.20). Here two relationships were considered, each tending to work in opposition to the other: (a) the company's not buying bulbs would reduce its costs but (b) if electric consumption dropped because consumers had to buy their own bulbs, costs of production might rise.

An overriding organizational principle (analysis 4.30) is implicit throughout, namely, the exclusion of influences not specified in the model. To cite just one such influence: if there occurs a momentous change in the technology of producing electricity—say, the use of atomic reactors—then all bets are off! No provision is made for so drastic an event. But, by ignoring this possibility which might upset all inferences, we implicitly assume technology as essentially fixed. The focus, then, is upon a selected change in a few relationships, excluding change in the art and science of electrical power generation.

Synthesis (5.00) of all that has gone before may be summed up as the entire economic analysis, the bulk of Chapter 6 (production of a unique communication, 5.10). To the extent that the discussion succeeded in shedding light on the light bulbs, the effort is a meaningful synthesis of those elements germane to the problem. (Obviously, "unique" here does not mean "highly original" nor "especially creative." The degree of the author's skill, or lack of it, would be an issue in these latter meanings of unique.)* A communication addressed to the question, Who pays for the light bulbs? is the result of the exercise of all skills earlier enumerated.

Finally we come to evaluation (6.00). This skill can be illustrated at

---

* We skip over Taxonomy items 5.20, production of a plan, and 5.30, derivation of a set of abstract relations. While a few inferences that were drawn could be included within the latter category, there seems little to be gained by doing so. The major point of the chapter was to synthesize an answer to the question earlier posed.

the level of fact by asking: How accurately does the number we have used measure the price of light bulbs? At the level of generalization—how well does the principle of profit-maximizing behavior fit the Detroit Edison Company? At the highest summary level—how well have we answered the question we set ourselves—who pays? Each of these questions, in turn, requires a more difficult evaluation. And the evaluation may be reached by the criterion of internal consistency (6.10) and by the criterion of consistency with external evidence (6.20). In the analysis of policy attempted in this chapter, only the former criterion was applied. That is, the validity of the conclusions was argued almost solely from the deduction that followed from the logic of the analysis itself; there was no attempt to cite the experience of other electric utilities to show by comparison what had happened when they adopted or abandoned a policy like the one practiced by Detroit Edison. There was no recourse to the extensive records of, say, the Federal Power Commission or the association of private utility companies. This would be an appeal to external evidence and, in a major research project, this appeal might be an essential step to take.

There are, of course, no hard and fast lines between any of the skills discussed here. Interpretation blends into application; synthesis may occur concurrently with evaluation. Yet in the use of knowledge, these skills are conceptually distinct and, in the study of any science or social science, the development of these skills is integral to the attainment of expertise. If we would know what to learn and what to teach, we need to identify these components of instruction. The objectives of curriculum can only be served by educators who have some reasonably clear ideas about how the objectives are defined. Only then does it become appropriate to plan the routes to their attainment.

Annotated Bibliography

Bloom, Benjamin S. (ed.), Max D. Englehart, Edward J. Furst, Walker H. Hill, and David R. Krathwohl, *Taxonomy of Educational Objectives. Handbook I: Cognitive Domain.* (New York: David McKay Company, Inc. 1956). A monumental attempt to classify learning of various disciplines into several categories of knowledge and skills. The book aims at clearer specification of curriculum objectives and is profusely illustrated with test questions and situations.

Bloom, Benjamin S., David R. Krathwohl, and Bertram B. Masia, *Taxonomy of Educational Objectives, Handbook II: Affective Domain* (New York: David McKay Company, Inc. 1964). Like its predecessor cited above, this handbook attempts the same thing in the area of affect: sensibilities, perception and awareness.

Bruner, Jerome L., *The Process of Education* (New York: Alfred A. Knopf, Inc., and Random House, 1960). Bruner's work, emphasizing the structure of knowledge of a discipline, has triggered controversy among educators. It is an excellent appreciation of the power of analysis in teaching and learning.

Calderwood, James D., *Developmental Economic Education Program*, Part One: "Economic Ideas and Concepts" (New York: Joint Council on Economic Education, 1964). Professor Calderwood develops herein the leading ideas set forth in the "Task Force Report" cited in this bibliography as *Economic Education in the Schools*. This little paperback is among the finest summaries of leading economic ideas.

Collingwood, R. G., *The Idea of History* (New York: Oxford University Press, 1946). I am told by historians that this is a profound work on the meaning of historical inquiry. My reading of the book leads me to agree with them.

Developmental Economic Education Program, Part Two: "Suggestions for Grade Placement and Development of Economic Ideas and Concepts" (New York: Joint Council on Economic Education, 1964). This document comes close to being a "scope and sequence" arrangement of leading economic ideas. It is best used in conjunction with DEEP Part One, cited elsewhere in this bibliography. The work is divided into four sections: elementary, junior high school, senior high school, and business education. This booklet and DEEP Part One were an important part of the curriculum efforts of 29 major school systems in the DEEP program.

Economic Education in the Schools, Report of the National Task Force on Economic Education (New York: Committee for Economic Development. September 1961). An excellent statement of the areas of application of economics requisite for economic literacy of high school graduates. It was prepared by a distinguished committee especially selected for this purpose.

Erikson, Erik, *Childhood and Society* (New York: W. W. Norton & Company, Inc., 1953). No brief annotation can do justice to the quality of Erikson's work. For present purposes I should emphasize the relevance of his discussion of outworn economic practice in impairing healthy human behavior.

Krug, Mark M., "Bruner's New Social Studies: A Critique," *Social Education*. Vol. XXX, No. 6, October 1966. The author represents an historical point of view in conflict with Collingwood, Ward, Bruner, Bloom, Whitehead, Robbins and Samuelson.

Peddiwell, J. Abner, *The Saber-Tooth Curriculum* (New York: McGraw-Hill Book Company, Inc., 1939, Paperback). A humorously incisive allegory showing how educators may teach what they teach because they have always taught it.

Riesman, David, *Constraint and Variety in American Education* (New York: Doubleday & Company, Inc., 1958, Anchor Paperback). Among Riesman's many valuable contributions, readers will be particularly interested in discussion of how different members of the academic community imitate the worn-out practices of other members who are deemed prestigious.

Robbins, Lionel, *An Essay on the Nature and Significance of Economic Science* (London: Macmillan & Co., Ltd., 1962). Largely microeconomic in spirit, this account is a clearly written exposition of the major contours of economic science.

Samuelson, Paul A., *Foundations of Economic Analysis* (Cambridge: Harvard University Press, 1947). This "classic" of economics is meant for economists with mathematical training. However, many sections of the text that are not mathematical deserve a wide reading because of the insights conveyed on the essential nature of economic inquiry.

Tyler, Ralph W., *Report on Cooperative Education* (Chicago: University of

Chicago Press, 1961 monograph). An excellent discussion of criteria useful to the selection of areas of study within the curriculum.

Walsh, Vivian Charles, *Scarcity and Evil* (Englewood Cliffs, N.J.: Prentice-Hall, 1961). An odd exercise in the moral implications of economic analysis, containing a peculiar novel set down in the middle of what is otherwise a philosophical treatment.

Ward, Paul L., "Should History Be Cherished? Some Doubts and Affirmations," *Social Education*, Vol. XXXI, No. 3, March 1967. A modern historian confirms several of the ideas of Bruner and Collingwood and contributes importantly to the teacher's understanding.

Whitehead, Alfred North, *The Aims of Education* (New York: The Macmillan Company, 1929). A provocative book long serving as a beacon to many educators.

Selected Bibliography of Instructional Material for Teachers and for Their Students

Bach, G. L., *Economics, An Introduction to Analysis and Policy*. Englewood Cliffs, N.J.: Prentice Hall, 1968. One of the leading college texts in principles of economics.

Econ LMN. Duluth, Minn.: Duluth Public School System, 1968. A series of six, 30-minute films dealing in delightful fashion with major economic ideas. It is addressed chiefly to teachers of elementary pupils.

Joint Council on Economic Education, *Checklist*. New York, N.Y. A listing of materials for both teachers and their students at all grade levels.

Lovenstein, Meno, *Capitalism, Communism, Socialism*. Chicago: Scott, Foresman & Co., 1962. An excellent book for high school students.

Samuelson, Paul A., *Economics: An Introductory Analysis*. New York: McGraw-Hill, 1967. Another of the leading college texts in principles of economics.

Waâge, Thomas D., *Money: Master or Servant?* New York: Federal Reserve Bank of New York, 1968. An analysis of money and banking for secondary school students.

The following books for students by John E. Maher and S. Stowell Symmes will be published in 1969 by Franklin Watts, Inc., New York, N.Y.

Ideas about Others and You. A simple explanation of social systems for early elementary pupils.

Ideas about Choosing. The problem of scarcity and the need for choice is discussed for early elementary pupils.

Learn about People Working for You. The interdependent economic system is explained for upper elementary students.

Learn about Why We Must Choose. An elaboration of the idea of scarcity and choice for upper elementary students.

Index

Accounting, 114, 119, 120
Aims of economics instruction, 133-139
Allocation, see Optimizing; Resources
American Economic Association, 8
Anthropomorphism, 110

Baruch, B., 60
Berdyaev, N., 143
"Best" solution, see Optimizing
Bloom, B. S., 153, 161
Borrowing, government, 6, 112, 113
Bruner, J., 48
Butz, O., 44
By-gones are bygones, 143

Calderwood, J. D., 50, 111
Choice, 45, 139; see also Optimizing; Scarcity
Circular flow of income, 5, 105, 110
Commons, J. R., 119

Competitive markets, 6; see also Efficiency
Competitive objectives, 49
Complementary objectives, 49
Consumer expenditures, 5, 101 103, 107, 110; see also Consumption
Consumption, 35, 36, 50
Consumption function, 107
Consumption relationships, 3, 27
Cost, 32, 78, 86, 111, 131-132
Council of Economic Advisers, 18
Criteria for curriculum, 133
Curriculum, criteria for, 133
    knowledge taxonomy and, 149-152
    skills taxonomy and, 153-159

DEEP, 149
Depreciation, 119
Detroit Edison Company, 76, 79, 91, 96-97

172   INDEX

Developmental Economic Education Program; *see* DEEP
Diminishing returns, 38, 50

Economics, accounting and, 114
 boundaries of, 128, 129
 causality in, 92
 curriculum and, 52, 133-139
 defined, 22-57
 history and, 142-144
 maturity of, 20
 misconceptions about, 58-75
 morality and, 139
 perspective, 22
 social policy and, 17, 75, 134
 structure of, 27, 52, 69
 taxonomy of, 153-159, 160-165
Economies of scale, 84-164
Economist consultants, 149-152
Economize, defined, 1, 26
 influence on behavior, 26
 see also Choice, Efficiency, and Resources
Efficiency, defined, 3, 6
 level of output and, 83
 optimal solution and, 39, 50, 68
 resource allocation and, 39, 42, 111
 technical versus economic, 37, 131
 Thoreau on, 57
Emerson, R. W., 147
Endogenous, 90
Equilibrium, 39, 40, 116; *see also* Efficiency, Maximizing
Erikson, E., 141, 142
Exogenous, 91

Federal Reserve System, 6, 17, 18
Fiscal policy, 6, 7, 18
Five features of economic activity, 49
 circular flow and, 101
 illustrated, 27, 28, 30, 79-82, 93
 limitations on, 54
 related together, 6, 30, 48
 stated, 2
Freud, S., 144, 145

Government, 5, 7, 112, 113; *see also* Federal Reserve System; Fiscal policy; and Monetary policy
Gross national product, 5, 7, 50, 122
Guideposts, 19

Highway safety and economic analysis, 14
History and economics, 142

Income, 109, 120; *see also* Gross national product; National income model
Input-output, 56, 74, 124
 defense and, 19
Institutional school, 115, 118
Instruction, 48; *see also* Curriculum

Jello, 13
Joint Council on Economic Education, 10, 149-152

Keynes, J. M., 106, 118
Knowledge, taxonomy of, 153-159

Lawrence, J. D., 73
Leontief, W., 19, 127
Liberal arts, 136
Linear flow, 101

Macroeconomics, 3, 50, 98
Materialism, 73
Mathematics, block to economists, 9, 66
 economics as, 65
 income determination, 107
 organizing economics, 115
 taxonomic illustrations of, 154
Maximizing, 41, 46, 111, 116; *see also* Efficiency; Equilibrium
Means and ends, 52
Microeconomics, 3, 27, 98
Minimizing, 46; *see also* Efficiency; Equilibrium; and Optimizing
Misconceptions of economics, 58-75
Mixed economy, 112
Monetary policy, 6, 7, 18

INDEX 173

Monopsony, 86
Morality and economics, 139; see also Choice; Scarcity
Multiplier, 109

National income model, 105, 108; see also Gross national product
National Task Force on Economic Education, 11
Noneconomic, 89

Objectives, 26, 27, 49, 66; see also Five features of economic activity
Opinion, economics as, 58
Opportunity cost, 35, 42; see also Efficiency
Optimizing, 32, 39, 42, 45, 46, 50
Organizations, perspectives on, 25
Outputs, 27, 49; see also Five features of economic activity

Phlogiston, 96
Pig philosophy, 74
Price, 3, 37; see also Cost
Problem solving as economics, 68
Production relationships, 3
Productivity, 100; see also Efficiency
Profit motive, 5
Profits, 46, 82, 111, 116, 121, 128, 154; see also Maximizing
Proverbs and economic analysis, 145
Psychoanalysis, 145
Public Service Commission, 85, 86, 94

Rationality, 26, 39, 42, 109
Real cost, 78; see also Opportunity cost
Relationships in economics, 48, 50, 93
  consumption, 3, 38
  price, 32, 37
  production, 3, 30, 37
Resources, allocation of, 34, 39, 41, 68
  income and, 106
  scarcity and, 1, 2, 6, 26, 30

Robbins, L., 13, 25, 74, 75, 117

Samuelson, P., 13, 115, 116
Santayana, G., 144
Satisfaction of wants, 33; see also Objectives; Wants
Saving, 4, 17, 109
Scarcity, 1, 6, 26, 64, 118, 139; see also Opportunity cost
Schumpeter, J., 13
"Sheer description," analysis versus, 23, 25
Skills, taxonomy of, 160-165
Social goals, 26, 44; see also Objectives
Sociology, 22, 24, 25
Spending, 4, 113; see also Consumer expenditures
Statistics and economics, 119
Stegosaurus, 13
Style and economics, 138
Substitution relationships, 38, 42, 50; see also Relationships in economics
Superlatives, erroneous use of, 43, 44, 45
Supply and demand, 118; see also Scarcity
System, 39, 91, 102, 125, 194; see also Five features of economic activity

Taxation, 6, 78, 92
Taxonomy, of knowledge, 153-159
  of skills, 160-165
Technical efficiency, 37; see also Efficiency
Technology, 13
Textbooks in economics, 9, 64, 65
Thoreau, H. D., 57
Topics as economics, 64
Trade, 62

Unemployment, 100
"Unlimited wants," 44, 70, 73

Values, 40, 131

Valuing human life, 15
Vending machine analogy, 4, 103, 105

Walsh, V. C., 139

Wants, 1, 6
　said to be unlimited, 44, 70, 74
　see also Objectives
Whitehead, A. N., 138